The Bedside Dream Dictionary

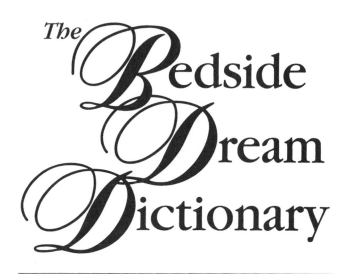

The Bedside Dream Dictionary

*Hundreds of Symbols to Unlock the
Mysteries of the Subconscious*

Silvana Amar

Skyhorse Publishing

Skyhorse Publishing books may be purchased in bulk at special discounts for sales promotion, corporate gifts, fund-raising, or educational purposes. Special editions can also be created to specifications.

For details, contact the Special Sales Department, Skyhorse Publishing, 307 West 36th Street, 11th Floor, New York, NY 10018 or info@skyhorsepublishing.com.

Skyhorse® and Skyhorse Publishing® are registered trademarks of Skyhorse Publishing, Inc.®, a Delaware corporation.

www.skyhorsepublishing.com

10 9 8 7 6 5 4 3 2

Paperback ISBN 978-1-62636-120-1

Library of Congress Cataloging-in-Publication Data
Amar, Silvana.
    The bedside dream dictionary / Silvana Amar.
p.cm.
    Includes bibliographical references and index.
    ISBN 978-1-60239-138-3 (pbk. : alk. paper)
    1.Dream interpretation—Dictionaries. 2.Dreams—Dictionaries.
I.Title.

BF1091.A49 2007
154.6'303—dc22
                                        2007016202

Printed in the United States of America

For my parents,
Josip and Stefica Ivin

Contents

Introduction

Dreams are the most direct path to the unconscious. They are an affirmation of the soul and a constant reminder that we are much more than our conscious thoughts and our current lives. Understanding dreams is beneficial for all people. Whether you consider yourself to be a pragmatic person or mystically inclined, understanding dreams will bring clarity and deeper meaning to your life.

In the dream state we have an opportunity to access both our private unconscious and the collective unconscious. According to Carl Jung, the primary functions of dreams are:

1. Dreams are a compensation for what is going on in daily life. They can serve as a positive or negative compensation. In this way, they attempt to balance the psyche. For example: If you experience unhappiness in daily life, you may have a blissful dream. If you are very successful in a specific area of life, you may have a dream about failure or disaster.

2. Dreams provide a reaction to a traumatic experience. For example: If you were in a car accident, you may dream of it and the dream may be a repeat of this negative experience. People who suffered great trauma, such as rape victims or war veterans, may have nightmares that are exactly like or very similar to actual life events. As the individual assimilates these traumatic

experiences, such dreams should become less and less frequent and may take another form.

3. Dreams may be prophetic. Some dreams may provide the dreamer with glimpses into the future about small matters, while other dreams may reveal important events. However, keep in mind that most dreams are symbolic and not literal. Prophetic dreams may have an emotional or psychic charge that is different from other types of dreams.

4. Dreams may be telepathic. In the American Heritage Dictionary, telepathy is defined as "communication through means other than the senses." Telepathic dreams may be a means of communicating with others, as well as a path for one part of the dreamer's psyche to communicate with another.

5. Dreams may be mimetic of events occurring in the physical system or body. Thus, dreams may attempt to bring to consciousness an unknown illness or be a reflection of a current physical challenge.

Understanding or interpreting dreams is not a simple task. The language of dreams is one of images and symbols; it is a foreign language. Learning it takes time, assistance, and perseverance. One may think of dreams as strange and unusual gifts. At times their messages may be obvious and at other times a mystery. Either way, they are a part of our humanity and divinity. Just as everyone sleeps, everyone dreams. Dreams may take us to our personal and private unconscious world, or connect us with all eternity in the collective unconscious realms.

Prologue

There are several different ways to interpret dreams. Dream interpretation depends on a person's belief system and their approach to interpreting dreams. It may be preferred to take a pragmatic approach and first look for real life causes for the dream. However, keep in mind that dreams can be interpreted on many different levels or depths. Dreams are something like onions—there are layers and layers—once you understand a dream's meaning on one level, underneath there may be another level or layer to interpret. The layer that you interpret and hold meaningful depends on the level or your awareness or consciousness. Dream interpretation is very personal and the meaning of symbols may depend on life experiences of the dreamer and his or her psychic needs. Also, keep in mind that many symbols are universal, in that they represent similar situations, issues, and challenges for all dreamers.

In order to develop a better understanding of your dreams, make an effort to keep a dream journal. It does not have to be extensive; upon awakening write down the most prevalent symbols, colors, and events in your dream. Additionally, try to remember the mood of the dream or your feelings in it. As you are writing in your journal you can begin writing your own personal dream dictionary. In the back of the journal, you may keep a list of the most outstanding or powerful dream symbols.

What is a dream symbol?

A dream symbol is an image from the unconscious that is important for you to understand in the present moment. Symbols can be understood subjectively and personal associations can be made to understand the dream's message. However, at times, the objective associations of the dream symbol may be more revealing and meaningful. For example, if dreaming about a ruby, you may have personal associations such as: I inherited my grandmother's ruby ring, or the ruby is my birthstone. These associations may be important, but if you consider the objective definition of a ruby it may bring you closer to the essence of the dream's message. Thus, a ruby is a precious stone harvested from deep within the earth. Historically, it represents healing and irrepressible light. With these associations, one may conclude that the dream has to do with inner wealth that may be harvested though introspection and that may bring about healing and enlightenment, or that the deepest level of healing is needed in the dreamer's life.

Each dream symbol may have multiple meanings and can be applied to many aspects of the dreamer's life. Thus, understanding the ruby dream with the use of subjective and personal associations may be meaningful and valuable on one level, but it may also have a wider and deeper meaning when looking at it with objective associations.

Dream Dictionary

From 1997 to 2004, a substantial number of people from all over the world, who had a computer and Internet access, logged on to a Web site and submitted requests for interpretations of dreams, and requests for meaning of specific dream symbols. Dream symbols included in this dictionary may be considered "living dream symbols" because they represent those things that people currently and most often dream about. If you cannot find a symbol that you are looking for, look at related symbols that may be in the dictionary. For example, if you dreamt about an orange and cannot find it in the dictionary, look up fruit, which will give you more general, but very helpful suggestions for interpretation. In the same way, if you dreamt about your grandmother who passed away two years ago, look up deceased relatives.

_A_

Abandonment

You must first consider this dream's varying aspects in order to interpret it. Your unconscious may be giving you messages regarding what needs to be kept and what needs to be let go. Traditional dream interpretations say that if you are the one being abandoned in your dream, it is a dream of the contrary and you may experience reconciliation or recovery from trouble or illness. Remember that the unconscious is attempting to compensate for an imbalance in the conscious. For example, if you are overly attached to someone in daily life, in the dream state he or she may abandon you. This is an attempt by the unconscious to make you aware of your dependency.

Abdomen

Dreaming about any body part is a way to bring the dreamer's conscious attention to it. When, in your dream, you are feeling pain or discomfort in this area or any other area of the body, consider how well that part of your body is functioning in real life. Being health-conscious is a positive thing and both psychological and physical factors need to be considered. At times our unconscious knows that something is wrong even before we have any symptoms. "Old wives' tales" tell us that this is a dream of the contrary and that you will have lots of vigor and good health.

Abortion

A woman that had this experience is most likely to have many dreams about it. Even though the dream may be disturbing or anxiety-provoking, it is a healing dream. It is possible that in your dream state you are working toward acceptance and are resolving any unconscious (and conscious) feelings. If a man is having this dream, it usually means that he is experiencing guilt feelings and may be anticipating failure of some kind. If a woman who has not had this experience is having this dream, it may be a warning about her health or may indicate that she is feeling significant anxiety about current endeavors.

Actor

Sometimes dreaming about a famous actor or actress may be a wish-fulfilling dream, or it could hold important messages about ourselves. We admire celebrities and may wish to have some of their characteristics. Consider the personality traits or any other trait that attracts you to that person. This will help you figure out why you are dreaming about him or her. If you are dreaming that someone is acting, you may be dreaming about yourself. The dream could be pointing out some of the roles that you play in life. Among the many roles we play are parent, spouse, lover, student, professional, etc. We behave somewhat differently in each of those roles. The actor in your dreams could be showing you how well you "play" some of your roles in life or how others perceive you.

Adultery

Many people seem to have dreams about committing adultery or about their spouse committing adultery (cheating or being cheated on). In this dictionary there is a definition for cheating and here I will add a few more thoughts about this dream topic. Many dreams come from the private unconscious and are a reflection on thoughts, fears, desires, or issues, or are a response to stressful or anxiety provoking situations. The details of the dream need to be considered before attempting an interpretation. Details such as who is cheating on whom and what are the circumstances surrounding this dream event need to be established. At times people have dreams about cheating on their spouses as a response to a long and monogamous relationship. The dream may be a compensation for boredom, monotony, or unhappiness. On the other hand, the dream could be about you connecting to deeper parts of self, which is represented by a desirable person of the opposite sex. On rare occasions a person may suspect, or feel on some level, that their mate is not faithful but is not willing to admit this consciously. Thus, in the dream state the individual confronts his fears and from there may begin to deal with the situation on a conscious level.

> *"The dream reveals the reality which*
> *conception lags behind."*
> —Franz Kafka

Aging

Dreaming about old people or your own aging may have several different meanings. An old man may symbolize wisdom and forgiveness while an old woman may represent life and death. In general, aging may represent the wisdom that a person acquires through experience. The dream may also be giving you a message in regard to life's lessons. This may be a good time for you to apply some of your experience and knowledge to a current situation. This dream may also be a reflection of your concerns about aging. If you are thinking about your mortality and do not welcome maturing and age, the dream may be bringing out some of your worries and/or vanities.

Airplane

We received an interesting amount of mail about dreams containing planes and plane crashes. It appears that people often dream about being in a plane crash, witnessing a crash, or being bombed or shot at from planes. Airplanes, like all other vehicles, symbolize a portion of your life's journey. The part of your life that is represented is usually a memory, material from your unconscious mind, or something that is physically far away from you. Since we use planes to travel to places that are far away, the logical progression of this interpretation is that the airplane is symbolic of an event, individuals, or emotions that are either in the past, physically apart from you, or deep in the unconscious and far from conscious thought. Disturbing dreams in which you are being bombed or where you see a bloody crash scene may be trying to bring up issues and feelings that have been buried in the unconscious mind (from the past or the present) but are still powerful and disturbing to you. The more powerful, vivid, and disturbing this dream is, the greater the necessity to interpret and obtain a satisfactory meaning. *See also:* Car, Travel

Alcohol

Understanding the symbol of alcohol in your dreams depends on the relationship you have with it in daily life. If you drink regularly, you need to look at the other details of your dream more carefully. However, if you drink rarely or never, then this dream could represent a need for you to escape from your daily stress and your desire to get quick relief. The alcohol could be suggesting a need for healing and getting in balance. Your unconscious mind may be suggesting outrageous things in hopes that you get the message to "have fun, dream dreams, and get out of your own head!" Please keep in mind that the purpose of dreams is to raise our consciousness and to assist us in having better lives. The message in the dream about alcohol is most likely not encouraging you to drink but it may represent a need to feel better or get better.

Alien

Occasionally, people will have dreams about UFOs and aliens. What these dreams symbolize, collectively or individually, is difficult to explain and understand. Meeting and talking to aliens may suggest that significant changes are coming into your life and, at the moment, things feel strange and foreign to you. If you dream that you are the alien, it suggests that you may feel detached from some parts of yourself and from others. You may be a stranger in your immediate surroundings, and some self-evaluation and familiarization is suggested.

Alligator

This cold-blooded animal could hold several different meanings in your dream. It could symbolically represent something from your memory, emotions, or a current situation or individual in your life. Some think that the alligator represents verbal power used in a destructive way (angry and hurtful words). Others believe that it represents an enemy. Consider the details in your dream and your level of fear. This dream symbol should encourage you to look at some of your more "dangerous" emotions, memories, and experiences. The alligators in your dreams will begin to lose the power to frighten you as your understanding increases. Carl Jung said that all wild animals indicate latent affects (feelings and emotions that we do not readily deal with). They are also symbolic of dangers (hurtful and negative things) being "swallowed" by the unconscious.

Ambulance

In old dream dictionaries, dreaming about an ambulance could be labeled as a dream of warning. From more modern perspective it could mean your unconscious mind is attempting to convey information that you have been unwilling to deal with consciously. Pay attention to your physical body and see if your health is an issue. Otherwise, this dream may be pointing to some urgent situation in your life. Consider all of the details in your dream. Examine your daily life and make an attempt to see if there is something that requires your immediate attention.

Amputation

This is a frightening dream which may be due to anxiety and fear. It suggests feelings of frustration, anger, and powerlessness on the part of the dreamer. This dream may also be related to a radical removal of something from one's life. Some believe that you are trying to get rid of something that is no longer desirable or necessary or that the limb or the part being amputated has lost its power. According to New Age thinking, the right side of the body is usually associated with the ability to give emotionally, psychologically and physically to yourself and others, while the left is linked with the ability to receive. Carl Jung said that the left side represents the unconscious while the right indicates the conscious

Amusement Park

This dream may be pointing to one of your perceptions about life or be symbolic of life itself. You may see some parts of your life as lively, interesting, adventurous and entertaining. On the other hand, depending on the details of the dream you may see yourself as being on a wild ride, where nothing is terribly serious and life is a perpetual "roller coaster ride." If you have been dealing with a significant amount of stress in your daily life or have been overworked, this dream may be a form of compensation. The dream's message may be to encourage you to find time for fun and relaxation as well as to remind you that life is full of ups and downs and that a light-hearted attitude may be a refreshing change.

Anchor

Dream interpretation is very personal and each dream speaks to you in the most intimate way. The anchor symbol could have varying meaning depending on what is going on in your life. It may be saying "Stay put!" or "This is a good place to lay down your anchor." Dreams involving anchors are hints from your unconscious and may suggest a need to reflect and economize.

Angels

In the past ten years there has been a renewed appreciation and interest in angels. They represent goodness, protection, and the heavenly realm. As a dream symbol they may attempt to focus the dreamer's attention on his own divine qualities and the supportive and loving aspects of life. Some say that dreaming about angels is a symbol of good luck, while others believe that you will see an angel in your dream around the time when there is a birth or death in your family, or in your close circle of friends. Angels are mystical and spiritual symbols; traditionally they have been the messengers of God. The interpretation of your dream angel depends on your own views. Generally, the message coming up from your unconscious may be of important magnitude, so record your dream and think about all of its details and implications.

Anger

This may be a carry-over from your daily life. In our dreams we can experience and express such feelings safely. Feeling great anger in your dream may be disturbing but pay attention to it and attempt to deal with all of your emotions in a more appropriate and productive manner. On a side note, many Jungian analysts believe that the emotions that we experience in dreams are not reliable, may have the opposite meaning, and in general should not be the only thing considered when interpreting a dream.

Animals

Carl Jung said that all wild animals indicate latent affects (feelings and emotions that we do not readily deal with). They are also symbolic of dangers (hurtful and negative things) being "swallowed" by the unconscious. The interpretation of the animal in your dream depends on your relationship with it in daily life. Animals represent the qualities in our character or specific aspects of our personalities. They could symbolize our more intuitive and instinctive parts, or they could serve as messengers for the unconscious. Please look up each animal individually by name.

Anxiety

Experiencing much anxiety in your dream state may be related to your current difficulties and everyday life. Gaps may exist between the way things are and the way you would like them to be. Older interpretation books suggest that when you dream about anxiety, the contrary is true and that your worries will be lessened. However, always keep the compensatory nature of dreams in mind. If you are not feeling anxiety during the day, it could be that you are ignoring it and that it will appear in your dream. Therefore, look at the details of your dream and attempt to identify the anxiety-provoking situations in your daily life.

Apology

This dream always has something to say about our relationships, the relationship that we have with ourselves and/or with others. Apologies are associated with forgiveness and honesty. Thus, consider the details of your dream and consider whether an apology is necessary in order for you to move forward in a particular relationship or with an area of your personal life.

Apple

This simple and basic fruit is a powerful symbol in religious writings, in literature, and in dreams. It fundamentally represents knowledge and the freedom that is associated with it. With knowledge and freedom we are in a position to make positive or negative choices. The apple should be interpreted with the consideration of all the other details in the dream. Is the apple a symbol of positive movement and spiritual and emotional liberation, or is it a symbol of runaway passions and the resulting negativity? Are you giving into temptation and making hurtful choices or are you being wise and enjoying the fullness of life?

Aquarium

Water in all forms is a very meaningful symbol. It may represent emotions, the unconscious, sexuality, and, at times, life itself. Before interpreting this symbol first consider the other details in the dream and the overall quality of the dream experience. The aquarium could represent a portion of your life or a "slice of life." Aquariums are generally balanced and fully contained ecosystems. People enjoy aquariums because they find them soothing and relaxing.

Thus, this dream's message may be a call for contemplation and relaxation. It may represent life in a small setting as a compensation to the stress and, at times, overwhelming complexity of daily experiences. *See also:* Water, Ocean, and River

Argument
See: Quarrel

Armor
Armor could represent your defense mechanisms, those things that you use to protect yourself from self or others (e.g., denial and repression). Physical barriers may keep others away, as will your more negative behaviors and attitudes. On a more spiritual note, some believe that dreaming about armor may be a good sign which represents a shield of protection from difficulties and temptation.

Arrow
The interpretation of this dream symbol may vary depending on whether the arrow was a tool or a weapon, or a sign-pointing direction. Dreaming about an actual arrow may have a range of meaning that includes swiftness, powerful and speedy intuition, mental alertness, precession, illuminating thoughts, and, last but not least, it could be a phallic symbol. To interpret the dream, consider its setting, context and emotional tone. Then, attempt to connect, and apply the suggested symbolism to your current situation or state of mind.

Attack

Research shows that the content of most dreams is more frequently unpleasant than pleasant. Most people have experienced violent dreams or dreams in which they are being attacked. To understand your dream, consider all of its details and think about whether you are the attacker or the one being attacked. If you are being attacked, then maybe you are feeling somewhat vulnerable in some area of your daily life. If you are doing the attacking, it may be that you are releasing some of your frustrations and anger while expressing negative feelings in ways that you are unable to do in daily life.

Attic

Any part of a house usually represents a part of yourself (dreamer = house). The attic is the last thing built. Consider the details of the dream and try to figure out what your unconscious is trying to tell you. Some believe that the attic symbolizes the higher self, or best self (i.e. the self that is in contact with the eternal). Others think that the attic symbolizes the sum total of your life's work or it may predict how well you will do in old age. If the attic is full of "neat" stuff, it may imply that you are accomplishing wonderful things and are living up to your potential in this lifetime.

Avalanche

The material which makes up the avalanche is snow, and snow is frozen water. Water symbolizes your emotions, the unconscious, and, at times, life itself. Therefore, this dream is about rapidly and violently descending emotions and thoughts. Emotions which may have been repressed have finally been unlocked and may be overwhelming you. You may have this dream during emotionally turbulent times of your life, or in your dreams you may be remembering and reliving some difficult emotional experiences. Old dream interpretation books say that burial in an avalanche may result in good luck in the near future. Therefore, they think that it is a dream of the contrary.

Ax

An ax is generally associated with destruction. We use it to break things up, and in popular horror movies it is used to kill people. The ax can also be used to carve and create art, furniture or other tools. A violent dream suggests that you may be experiencing frustration, anger and hostility. If there was no violence in your dream, then the ax may be positively interpreted as a symbol of productivity and creativity. Either way, an ax is a powerful tool, and as a dream symbol it may be saying something about your personal power and its expression.

Baby

Many people from time to time will have babies or small children in their dreams. If these newborns are strangers to you, you can assume that they represent you. You are the baby and the dream is telling you something about your development in a particular area of your life. At times of great change and renewal, a baby may appear in a dream and represent your potential and a new beginning. Some of the meaning of the dream may be obtained by considering what the baby looked like and was doing. Generally, babies represent innocence and are symbols of the purest form of a human whose possibilities are endless. However, if the baby's appearance is odd, and if your interactions with it are bizarre or unusual, you need to consider your own well-being (psychologically) and think about what personal experiences and psychological hang-ups have prevented you from growing.

Bake

When we bake, we transform matter. We take raw materials and make them into something nutritious and pleasing. Dreaming about baking is a positive dream image. It suggests that you are feeling optimistic and productive.

Bald

Some believe that dreaming about baldness is a warning about poor health. However, baldness symbolizes a lack of something, just like those who are bald lack hair. Hair represents feelings of personal power and beauty. Consider if such issues are currently relevant in your life.

Bananas

Freud suggested that all such objects have phallic implications. However, all types of food bring up issues of nourishment. In the world of classic or superstition-based dream interpretations, eating bananas suggests a period of hard work but little reward. Spoiled fruit usually suggests "spoiled" situations or friendships.

Bar/Pub

When I was in college, I read in a theology book that a monk on a mountain top and a man with his bottle of wine are really trying to get to the same place. That "place" translates to peace and a genuine feeling of being connected to the rest of the universe. Dreaming about being in bars and drinking may symbolize a need that you have for some type of a meaningful transformation. On the other hand, this dream may be a form of wish fulfillment, and you are escaping into a pleasurable environment where daily cares and concerns are meaningless. If you rarely allow yourself to relax and socialize, this dream may be compensatory in nature.

Basement

The house generally represents your psychological and emotional self. Each part of the house may deal with a different part of you. The basement is built first. It is often below ground (or at least some parts of it), and is essentially the foundation of the house. Dreaming about a basement and understanding the dream may provide you with valuable information that may lead to greater self-awareness. A recurring dream about basements (i.e., being in a basement, cleaning a basement, furnishing a basement, etc.) should not be ignored. These dreams may be symbolic of your unconscious, instincts and intuition, and degree of awareness of a current situation or a problem. The look of the basement may provide you with clues about your current feelings and state of contentment. If the basement is a mess, and you see great disorder and clutter, it suggests that you may be experiencing confusion and that it is a very good time to "sort" things out emotionally and psychologically. At times, the activities in the dream basement may be based on past experiences or childhood memories. As with all dreams, their main purpose seems to be to bring the dreamer to higher consciousness so that he may deal with his current issues more effectively, rather than dwell on the past. *See also:* House

Bat

Most bats are nocturnal predators and just thinking about these mysterious creatures gives most people an uneasy feeling (unless you are a bat lover). Bats may be considered mysterious and unpredictable. When you are interpreting this dream, look carefully at the details and your emotional reactions to the events in the dream. This dream may be related to discrete or covert behaviors. Your unconscious mind may be relating feelings to you in regard to behaviors that you or someone else prefers to keep a secret.

Bath

Taking a bath in a dream may represent your need to undergo some form of cleansing. If you are currently changing things in your daily life, or if you have freed yourself from bothersome emotions, this dream may be an affirmation of that. Taking a bath represents a cleansing of the outer self, the washing away of those things that are difficult or disturbing and relaxing for a while. The deeper meaning may be that the bath represents the letting go of old and useless ideas, opinions, or prejudices. Often this dream is a call to relax, to free your mind of daily troubles, and to put your problems away for a while. *See also:* Water

Bathroom

Dreaming about bathrooms seems to be common. They are most valuable in our daily life. In our dreams bathrooms may be equally valuable symbols. They suggest that there is a need for emotional and psychological cleansing. You may need to get rid of emotional and psychological baggage. It is difficult to be carefree and happy when old issues keep "bringing you down." The bathroom is a good dream symbol. Consider all of the details in your dream. Make an effort to cleanse mind and spirit by putting useless thoughts and feeling behind you. *See also:* House

Beard

Beards are usually associated with masculinity, wisdom, strength; and the men who have them typically command respect. Moses, Jesus, Charles Darwin, and Abraham Lincoln all had beards. Old dream interpretation books say that dreaming of bearded men is a good omen, and good luck will follow. On the other hand, dreaming about women with beards is said to be bad luck. It's no wonder that traditionally a woman who is strong, wise, and who commands respect was considered threatening. If you are a woman dreaming that you have a beard, you may be dealing with your own issues of power. You may be using more masculine energy than you would like to or than is necessary. Also, since beards conceal the faces of those who have them, they may symbolize negative characteristics, such as deception, extreme guardedness, or of the shadow (Bluebeard, a folktale by Charles Perrault). *See also:* Hair

Bears

A bear in a dream is a very rich and complicated dream symbol. In order to understand it, objective associations need to be made. Bears are solitary animals and the females are solitary mothers. They hibernate in a cave and they are generally not predatory animals. A bear is only aggressive when provoked, and at such times he is dangerous and deadly. Bears in dreams may represent a period of introspection and depression. However, this may be a part of a healing cycle, where the dreamer has retreated into himself in order to regenerate and in order to create something new and valuable in his life. Bears are highly regarded symbols in a variety of cultures and traditions, including the Native American tradition. Carl Jung said that all wild animals represent latent affects (feelings and emotions). The interpretation of the bear in a dream may be influenced by your perception of it and by the events in the dream. The bear may represent qualities in your character or specific aspects of your personality. Bears are usually associated with danger and aggression, but this is a very narrow view of this powerful dream symbol.

Beaver

Beavers are very busy animals. They gnaw all day and build their homes. They are generally not considered to be friendly animals. All of their hard work is focused on isolating and protecting themselves. When dreaming about these animals, consider those characteristics and try to see how they are relevant to you or someone in your life. Is there isolation and "blocking" up of feelings and self-expression going on around you? Or is something "gnawing" at you that you can no longer ignore? If you can answer these questions, you will have a better understanding of your dream.

Bed

This is one of the most valued pieces of furniture. It's where we sleep, rest, restore our minds and bodies and engage in sexual pleasure. The bed is symbolic of all of these things. The bed could also symbolize the bridge between the conscious and the unconscious (i.e., our daily lives and the great unknown, our spirit and our psychological undercurrent). The quality and the cleanliness of the bed in our dreams, may say something about the way we feel about our relationships and ourselves. In reality we "make our own bed," so the dream may reflect that bed and remind us that we have to either change it or lie in it. If there were things hiding under the bed in your dream, it may symbolize secrets that you or others are keeping.

Bees

Consider the details of this dream, as well as your emotional reactions in it, as bees can have a variety of different connotations. The positive symbolism is that of a person who is

hard working, has good organizational skills, and is coopera-
tive and creative. The negative symbolism could be that of a
follower, a busybody, or someone who "stings." If you are
working on a project in which many people need to work
together to accomplish a goal, this may be a topic for some
of your dreams.

Bicycle

All vehicles symbolize our passage through the journey of
life. Since the bicycle is usually acquired earlier in life than a
car, it could be pointing out some of your adolescent tendencies. If you are a teenager, then it may be a routine way
of getting around. Riding a bicycle in your dream may symbolize a need for balance and hard work in order for you to
succeed in a current endeavor. Some think that the bicycle
could also represent your need for some type of assistance.
Consider all of the details in your dream, including whether
you are traveling up or down the road. *See also:* Car, Road,
Journey

Birds

Carl Jung said that birds represent thoughts while birds in
flight symbolize moving and changing thoughts. Birds are
generally associated with freedom and abandon. In old
dream interpretation books, birds are considered lucky
omens (except for blackbirds, which are generally negative). Doves and eagles are generally spiritual symbols. Your
dream depends on its details, but if the birds in your dream
were flying free, it may be symbolic of spiritual, psychological, or physical freedom.

Birth

Women who are pregnant and men who are going to be fathers commonly have dreams about giving birth. It is not an omen of anything to come, but simply the mind trying to cope with a significant anxiety-provoking event. If you or your mate is not pregnant, this dream could symbolize new beginnings (i.e., giving birth to new ideas, new ways of living, or a new stage in life). Superstition-based dream interpretations say that giving birth in a dream is a sign of good luck, while multiple births are omens of forthcoming material wealth.

Blindness

Those who are literally blind cannot see the world around them. They can only perceive images with their mind's eye. When the dream is about being blind, the message is of a psychological and spiritual nature. Blindness in a dream suggests that the dreamer may be unwilling to see some aspect of his life. There may be a blind spot in the mind, heart, or soul; the unconscious material being processed by the dream threatens the dreamer and he cannot bring it to his conscious attention. The good news is that dreams are cyclical in nature. A message that cannot get through at the current time will repeat itself at a future date. The very central point of dreams is to make us aware of all aspects of ourselves and our lives; enlightenment and integration of unconscious and conscious components take time and desire. What you cannot see in a dream currently will become visible when you are more able to effectively cope with the message. This definition also applies to darkness and sleep as dream symbols.

Blood

It is the life-giving, vital part of our physiology and it may symbolize our strengths and weaknesses and our physical and mental health. If you are currently experiencing a very difficult time in your life, you may have dreams with bloody and frightening images. Don't worry: you may be venting your fears! Some believe that when you see blood in your dream, the distressing situation in your life, which is at the root of the dream, has come to an end, and the worst is over. Consider the details and the relationships between all of the symbols in your dream before making an interpretation.

Boat

As mentioned in all relevant entries, bodies of water represent your unconscious, your emotions, and your accumulated soul experiences. Depending on the content of the dream, several different interpretations could be made. The boat in your dream could represent you and the manner you navigate through your emotions. It could symbolize the voyage of your life, an adventure and exploration of your unconscious, or a connection to the people in your dream by pointing out something that all of you have in common ("in the same boat"). When interpreting this dream, consider the kind of voyage and the type of boat. Superstition-based dream interpretation books say that if the voyage is calm, you should go forward with your plans. However, if it is a very stormy voyage, get ready for an emotional upset (or challenge).

"...But O the ship, the immortal ship! O ship aboard
the ship! Ship of the body, ship of the soul,
voyaging, voyaging, voyaging."
— Walt Whitman

Body

Dreaming about your body generally suggests that you are dreaming about your personal identity. Who we are is wrapped around what we look like. Our self-esteem and self-worth are too frequently dependent on our physical appearance. This dream may be pointing out some of the difficulties or pleasures in daily life that are the result of self-identity and based on attachment to our physical bodies. The body in general is the symbol of self, and the details in the dream will lead you to further interpretation. Additionally, if you are dreaming of a specific body region, or part, consider your health status.

Books

In our daily life, books are a source of information and a place to gain knowledge. They can be inspirational, and their messages are sometimes so strong that they change our lives. The books in our dreams can represent our memories, learned understanding, ideas, or viewpoints. They can alert us to the fact that we have something new to learn and that we should spend time on mastering new tasks. Pay attention to what kind of book you are seeing in your dream and its purpose in the larger context of the dream. Also, note reading any passages or specific messages from the book. At times the book may be pointing to new themes or purposes in your life. Pay attention! The unconscious mind is constantly making attempts to communicate with the conscious in such ways that the dreamer will recognize it without panic or denial. Superstition-based dream interpretations say that if you are dreaming of books, you can be assured of slow but steady progress in your life. *See also:* School, Library

Box

A box is believed to be a feminine symbol that represents the unconscious, the mysterious, and the maternal. The famous Pandora's box held all the forces of good and evil in it. Pandora opened the box and unleashed its wrath into the world. She was able to close the box and in it hope. Thus, it is said that hope remains. (Pandora's box was not really a box at all, but a jar!) The interpretation of the box in your dream depends on the details of the dream and on the content of the box. Just remember that the box is symbolic of mystery, secrecy, and of something precious. The box in your dream might represent potential that needs to be realized and that will slowly come to your conscious awareness. Dreaming of a box suggests that risk taking may be necessary and that you may discover power and wealth that currently may be in the unconscious.

Bread

As a food, bread is a fundamental part of most diets. In poverty bread is the filler, and in jail the prisoner receives bread and water to keep from starving. In Christianity, Christ is the "bread of life," and in popular jargon bread may refer to money. Cross-culturally in both physical and metaphysical references, bread is the basic sustenance of life. As a dream symbol it is rich in both meaning and message. The bread in your dreams could represent those positive and wonderful things that you have learned in your life's journey. It could be symbolic of "good" and most basic things in your life that will yield positive benefits in the future. The bread in your dream could be spiritually symbolic; it could represent a profound communion or connection with others and with God. Consider the details of your dream before interpreting, but know that bread has positive universal symbolism and that this dream should bring with it a level of positive feelings and peace.

Breasts/Breast Feeding

Dreaming about breasts can have obvious sexual meaning. However, consider all of the details in your dream in order to obtain the most appropriate meaning. Breasts also represent tenderness, love, and other matters of the heart. Breastfeeding is symbolic of giving or receiving, nurturing, and sustenance. It represents motherly love as well as physical and emotional support and well being. Old dream interpretation books say that breastfeeding is a symbol of great things to come following an extended period of hard work.

Bridge

There are many meanings that you could give to this symbol. The details in the dream are just as important as the bridge itself. The first consideration should be given to how much you travel. The bridge can be interpreted literally if it is a part of your daily commute. On a more theoretical level, bridges can symbolize transitions (e.g., transition from one stage to another, from one level of consciousness to another). Since most bridges are over water (i.e., emotions, unconscious), this dream could also be symbolic of your rising above your emotional difficulties or unconscious drives.

Brown

Brown is not the most cheerful color in the spectrum. It is a very serious color that is associated with the earth, dirt, or soil. Autumn is generally brown and it represents a season of dormancy and conservatism. The brown in your dream may be symbolic of physical reality and earthiness. It may represent things in their "barest" form, and its interpretation may encourage you to add some light and depth into your daily life. *See also:* Colors

Bull

Depending on the details of the dream, this dream symbol could have several different meanings. The bull in your dream could represent powerful sexual energy, stubbornness, strength, and, at times, clumsiness. It could also symbolize optimism about the future and an ability to focus on a specific goal. Bulls can represent tenacity and a very strong will. Finally, since the bull is associated with the color red, some believe that it symbolizes the first chakra, which is the energy center located at the base of the spine and represents this material world.

Burial

Dreaming about funerals or burying a dead person does not necessarily symbolize physical death for you or anyone else. It could instead symbolize an ending of a different kind. You may be burying relationships, conditions, or even emotions that you no longer need and which are no longer conducive to your personal growth. On the other hand, this dream may symbolize the burying of sensitivities and emotions that are too difficult to cope with. It may reflect numbness or a feeling that is the opposite of vivacity, such as depression and emptiness. Either way, burying a living person suggests some emotional turmoil. Please consider all of the details in this dream to find the appropriate message. Old dream interpretation books say that dreaming about burials is a dream of the contrary. Instead of sadness the dreamer will experience happiness and go to celebrations, such as weddings. *See also:* Coffin, Death

Bus

In order to interpret the dream with a bus ride in it, the dreamer should make associations in regard to buses. The dream has very specific meaning depending on the individual's experiences on school buses, public transportation vehicles, special family trips, etc. At times the content of the dream may be more important than the actual setting. If the setting is secondary, then examine the other details of the dream more closely. However, if the bus, or the bus ride, was a focal point of the dream consider the value that it holds for you. Does this dream say something about your ability to "fit in" and join a group effort, project, or trip? Do you function well in group settings? Are you a leader or a follower in such situations, and what is your comfort level? This dream could also reflect a part of your life (or the journey of your life) that involved many other people who seemed to be on a same path. It could be your family, friends, schoolmates, or co-workers. *See also:* Car

Butterfly

Some say that the butterfly represents the spirit or the essence of the individual: the soul. Butterflies are generally symbols of transformation because they go through a metamorphosis. They are beautiful, evasive, and, at times, inspiring. Your unconscious mind may be pointing out the most positive part of yourself or another.

Buttons

Most often the button in your dream is a button on a piece of clothing, rather than a button that you push. Buttons on clothing represent something from your physical, or outer, self. Note if you were buttoning or unbuttoning, and, from there, attempt to obtain meaning. Unbuttoning generally represents an opening up of your emotions or ideas. You may be leaving yourself open to new possibilities as you are letting go of old thoughts and ways of doing things. Alternatively and on a positive side, buttoning up may reflect a need to conserve and to pull inward, to "button" your lip or to restrain yourself in some way. The more negative interpretation of buttoning up may be that you are currently feeling bound, restricted, or lacking some type of freedom.

Cage

This dream symbol suggests that you may be experiencing inhibition and powerlessness in some areas of your life. Additionally, you may be feeling restricted and have concerns about your personal freedom. (Who holds the key to the cage in your dream?) Consider all of the details in the dream and look for its possible source (i.e., family life, relationships, thoughts and/or feelings, or work life).

Cake

It may symbolize the sweet and pleasurable parts of life. The dream may be interpreted according to your interaction with the cake in the dream.

Calculator

See: Numbers, Machinery, Money

Cancer

Dreams are symbolic and not literal—most of the time. Cancer tumors in dreams represent a variety of unprocessed psychological and emotional materials that the dreamer may be obsessing on; they represent all of those things that bother, disturb, anger, or hurt us and that we never directly deal with or let go of. The dreamer's mental, psychic, or emotional problems may be proliferating and infecting many areas of thought and function. You may be experiencing anxiety and fear as a result of a bad habit or a certain situation in your daily life. However, if you are very worried and cannot get it out of your mind, go for a physical. When is the last time you did that anyway? In more superstitious interpretations, dreaming of cancer may be considered a dream of the contrary, but also of warning!

Candles

They symbolize light, and where there is light, there is hope. A lit candle suggests that you are unconsciously seeking comfort and some sort of spiritual enlightenment. An unlit candle suggests that you may be feeling rejection and disappointment or can't see anything positive or "light" in a situation or in yourself. If in your dream you watch the candle burn down to nothing, it suggests that you may have fears of getting older and dying. For men it may connote a fear about waning sexual abilities.

Cannibalism

This dream may reflect dark, destructive, and forbidden desires or obsessions. Cannibals literally consume other people's lives and, along with it, their energy. When interpreting this dream, consider those things that consistently drain you and take away from your enthusiasm and the general quality of your life. It may be any number of things, such as career or a relationship. However, realize that you are not a victim of life, but rather its creator. Thus, make changes that will increase your energy, but not take away from others. Some believe that dreaming about cannibalism is warning the dreamer to stay away from things that are destructive and less than honorable.

Car

The car in your dream may symbolize the physical self or ego development and ego function. In that, it represents the way that you travel through your life's journey. Consider all of the details in the dream, including its emotional content (i.e., difficulty of the road, identity of the driver, direction of the incline). Recurring car dreams usually deal with life's major themes that may include issues of control and sensibility. By carefully examining this dream, you may gain insight into important areas of life, including how well you are navigating from one stage of your life to another, if you are assertive and take charge or are passive. Dreaming about traveling in a car is a very, very common dream theme that provides valuable information in regard to a specific part of or long-standing theme in your life's journey. *See also:* Journey, Road

Carnival

See: Amusement Park

Cartoon

Seeing a cartoon world in your dreams or seeing cartoon-like people suggests that your unconscious is sending up messages which are telling you something about the way you perceive the world. The cartoon people, or cartoon characters, suggest that you may perceive yourself and those around you as comical or as not having much validity or seriousness. Your perceptions may be somewhat off due to your inability to look at the way things really are. Your mind's eye distorts things so that you are more comfortable with what is going on around you. If your world is full of stress and this dream made you laugh, consider the compensatory nature of it. In your dream you may be able to obtain moments of lightheartedness and fun.

Castle

A castle in a dream may be symbolic of the "cavern of the heart." It represents the home of the human spirit (yours) and the natural self. Dreams with castles in them may come from deeper levels of the unconscious, or the collective unconscious. They may represent spiritual transcendence and the mysterious and intangible force that seems to quietly, but firmly, direct our lives. A castle in a dream may also represent feelings of security, protection, isolation or remoteness. You may have a castle dream when you have realized a desire or accomplished a goal. Darkened castles may be symbolic of unconscious or unfocused desires; at times, black castles represent our failures and white, or lighted castles, symbolize achievement and awareness.

Cat

Cats have both positive and negative connotations. You need to consider all of the details in the dream in order to obtain accurate interpretation. The cat can be a symbol of sexuality, femininity, prosperity, and power. A cat is also an independent animal, and in your dream you may be associating yourself or someone else with these characteristics. Usually the dream is telling you about yourself and not others. Historically black cats have been symbols of evil and bad luck. If you are a cat lover and have one as a pet, the symbolism may not apply to your dream. Old, superstition-based dream interpretations say that a cat is a bad omen and that you can expect deceit from those who you trust.

Caterpillar

This bug may represent a stage in your own personal growth and development. The butterfly is a symbol of transformation; it represents a level of individual achievement. The caterpillar, on the other hand, may indicate that you are on your way but have not reached your goal. You may be in earlier stages of accomplishing a real-life goal, a relationship goal, or even a spiritual goal. The caterpillar may represent a specific area of your life or may be symbolic of the larger you.

Cave

Caves are rich and thought-provoking dream symbols. At times, a woman with reproductive issues may have a cave dream, in which case it represents the womb. The cave, as the womb, can represent new life, creativity, warmth, and safety. The cave can be a general symbol of a safe place, a sanctuary or a refuge. If you are experiencing much anxiety in daily life, in your dream state you may retreat to a warm cave where you cannot be disturbed by worldly demands. The cave could also represent the mysterious and unexplored parts of self. It could be symbolic of the unconscious mind, which could be a pleasant or a frightening experience. Your personal associations and experiences with caves, as well as the details and the emotional content of this dream, need to be carefully considered before making an interpretation.

Celebrity

See: Actor

Cemetery

A cemetery is a collection of dead organic matter. It is a sad and depressing place that doesn't reflect any joy, and reflects even less hope. Dreaming about cemeteries may be a reflection of your mood or unresolved grief. It may literally represent sadness that comes from losing someone that you love, or it could represent your past and long-gone experiences. *See also:* Graveyard

Chase

Folklore interpretations say that if you are looking at a chase or participating in it, you will have a comfortable old age. Although this may be comforting, there is a more realistic understanding of this activity in a dream. For example, if you are being chased maybe you are running away from and trying to escape things that are frightening and unpleasant (possibly your own habits and negative behaviors). If you are doing the chasing, it may be that you are expressing some aggressive feelings toward others or are pursuing a very difficult goal. On the deepest level, if a stranger is chasing you it may represent your chasing a part of yourself, the unconscious attempts to catch up with the conscious in order for you to become more aware of yourself and your own multidimensional nature.

Chewing Gum

For several years now, I have been learning about similar dreams from people all over the world. The dreams are almost exactly the same and involve the dreamers' inability to get rid of chewing gum. The more they attempt to remove it from their mouths the larger and more unmanageable it becomes. In the dream they become frustrated and panicky because the harder they try to pull, the larger the mass becomes in their mouths. This dream suggests that the dreamer may experience frustration in daily life due to a large scale or standing insolvable problem that leaves them feeling powerless. The dream represents an inability to digest or to process information or a dilemma. It also suggests that the dreamer is not able to express him or herself effectively and that repetitive and ineffective verbal expressions are typically used. Chewing gum in dreams may be a sign of childlike behaviors, vulnerability, powerlessness, and a need for nourishment.

Chickens

This flightless bird may be pointing to personal characteristics and needs that you may not necessarily want to look at. Consider the activities in the dream, as well as the mood, and then attempt to make a good interpretation. Chickens can represent cowardliness, gossip, excessive talking, and powerlessness. They are not known for their intelligence or beauty, and their presence in your dream could be an invitation to get more serious and better focused. The more positive suggestion in this dream is that chickens lay eggs. Eggs are symbolic of something new and fragile. They represent life and development in its earliest forms and as such, their possibilities are limitless.

Child

Some people have reoccurring dreams about a small child, while others, from time to time, dream about unfamiliar children. The child in your dream could represent your inner self, or the child within. The dream could be based on childhood memories, and it may carry a specific message or bring up long-buried issues. On the other hand, the dream could simply be a pleasant memory. Children in dreams could symbolize a need and an eagerness to learn, simplicity, intuition, new endeavors, and many other positive attributes of childhood. Occasionally, the child in your dreams may be pointing to your own childish ways. Therefore, consider all of the details and the tone of the dream before making an interpretation.

Choking
See: Smothering

Church
Dreaming about being in a church is more common than most people realize. Each week I get several requests to add church to the dictionary. This may be due to the fact that most of us went to church as children. From a very early age we had to go to church and were taught that there is a God. This was important in our life and to our families. Dreaming about churches, cathedrals, synagogues, or any other place of worship may represent our childhood associations with religion. At times, the dream may be a muddled childhood memory. The church could represent a need for greater spirituality in the dreamer's life. It may express religious beliefs, everyday occurrences, issues of safety, security, and strength through community and religious expression. None of us can escape the age-old questions such as "Who am I?" and "What is the meaning of life?" Coping with our own physical mortality is a very big deal. Both our con-

scious and unconscious minds are continually working and bringing issues of relevance and concern into our awareness. Think about the details of your dream and make an attempt to honestly understand its meaning.

Cigarettes

The interpretation of this symbol, as with all others, depends on your relationship with cigarettes. If you are a smoker or are surrounded by smokers, cigarettes may be a regular part of your daily life that has been brought into your dream state. Cigarettes could represent anything from phallic symbols and symbols of pleasure to tools of destruction. Generally, the cigarette is an object that carries social and emotional significance. When we are teenagers, we associate them with being "cool," daring, and defiant. For some adults they become a way of life where all emotions seem to be punctuated with cigarettes. Finally, as adults come into touch with their own physical mortality, cigarettes become dreadful objects, and smoking becomes a terrible burden and curse. When interpreting the dream with cigarettes in it, ask yourself what cigarettes mean to you. *See also:* Smoking

Circle

The circle symbolizes infinity, the circle of life and the eternal unknown. You, the dreamer, may have come to a greater degree of spiritual awareness, so the dream could be spiritual in nature. Carl Jung called most circular images a "mandala." It is one of the most important dream symbols that represent the psychic center of personality. It is symbolic of wholeness, completeness, and unity of the self. However, as always, examine all of the details in the dream, as well as its tone and mood, and rule out the possibility of "going in circles" as the primary message in the dream.

Cliff

Standing on the edge of a cliff could be a frightening but at the same time exhilarating experience. Dreaming about cliffs generally indicates that the dreamer has come to a point of heightened understanding and awareness. An increase in the level of consciousness may have occurred. Through hard work and perseverance, the dreamer may have reached a vantage or plateau of understanding.

Climbing

Going upward, or ascending, is always a positive dream symbol. Whether you are struggling on a difficult rope or ladder or walking up an easy slope, this dream suggests that you are moving in the right direction. If the climb in your dream is extremely difficult, it may be pointing to some obstacles that you need to overcome before reaching your goals. Consider all of the details in your dream, and if you recently completed a difficult task, achieved a goal, this dream may be reflective in nature. *See also:* Cliff

Clock

Circular images are one of the most important dream symbols, which represent the psychic center of personality. They are symbolic of wholeness, completeness, and unity of the self. The clock is a mandala that revolves and it may represent immortality. On the lighter side, when you are dreaming about a clock, time is an obvious issue. You may be currently experiencing anxiety in regard to a time-sensitive situation. For example, people worry about their "biological clock" running out, or they are concerned about not being "on top of things." In general, however, this dream may be a reminder that you need to speed up your actions and that time is an important factor. Old dream interpretations say that if you hear a clock strike, or an alarm go off, positive things will happen to you, and if you are winding a clock, you will fall in love! When interpreting this dream, try to remember the time and then attempt to understand how those numbers are meaningful to you.

Closet

The closet in your dream may have emotional, psychological, or physical connotations. Closets are used to store good things that we need as well as useless stuff. Emotionally they hold memories, secrets, precious emotions, and valuable thoughts. Consider all of the details in your dream and try to see the message clearly. Do you need to clean out the closet, come out of the closet, or share the things that you have stored in that closet?

Clothing

Clothing generally represents our worldly appearance or status. At times, it may represent our attitudes toward others and ourselves. Mostly, it represents the way that we appear to the world. Clothes are not symbolic of our private self, but rather of our public self. A poor man wears different clothes than a rich man. A doctor's attire is different from that of a carpenter. The type of clothing that we wear varies from situation to situation. The type of clothes that you are wearing

in the dream will give you clues to the meaning of the dream
and to your unconscious ideas about yourself and others.

Clouds

Clouds are made of air and water, two of the four basic elements. Some would say that the soul is represented by air
and spirit by water. Your positive energy and idealism could
be represented by white clouds and your more negative personal characteristics, and private thoughts, by dark storm
clouds.

Cockroaches

Cockroaches usually make people feel squeamish and re-
pulsed. When dreaming about these dreaded insects, the unconscious mind may be hinting to the dreamer that he
needs to reevaluate and reassess a major part of his life.
There is never just one roach; thus, the areas of life that
need cleansing and renewal may be deep and wide. The
negativity or contamination that is represented by the
roaches may affect a great deal of your life. Thus, this may
be a call to clean your psychological, emotional, and spiritual self. (Also, examine your motives!) On a less dramatic
note, cockroaches in our dreams may be associated with
food and a lack of cleanliness, so don't leave the dishes for
tomorrow!

Coffin

Coffin as a dream symbol most likely evokes fear, but before
making a quick interpretation, carefully consider all of the
details of the dream. The coffin could symbolize a lack of
energy or vitality in the dreamer. It could represent the

death of one stage of life and movement into another. (Not necessarily physical death! In fact, some cultures believe that if you see a person dead and in a coffin, he will most likely live a long and healthy life!) When dreaming about coffins, we may be contemplating the nature of the death experience and may access the state of consciousness that is attuned to the spiritual world. Most simply, and most likely, the coffin in your dreams may represent feelings of confinement and lack of freedom. *See also:* Burial, Death

Colors

Most people dream in colors, but at times some stand out more than others. Colors are symbolic and their symbolism is part of culture. We communicate with color and relate ideas with them. For example, a bride wears white and black is worn at funerals. Colors also represent energy. The meaning that you give to the colors in your dreams depends on the meaning that you give to those colors in daily life. If you "see red" when you are angry, then red symbolizes anger and not passion for you. Some generalizations have been made as to the meaning of colors in dreams. They are as follows:

Black—depression, sadness, and despair. Some believe it symbolizes hidden sexual desires.

Blue—spirituality, optimism, positive thoughts, communication. Some believe that when you see it in your dreams, you may be in the presence of your spiritual guide.

Green—money, jealousy, health concerns, love.

Red—passion, sexuality, anger, warning.

White—purity, transformation, cleanliness, dignity.

See also: Pink, Yellow, Brown, Purple, and Orange

Couch

Dreaming about a couch could mean that you may have a need for some rest and relaxation. The couch also has other symbolism. For example, it could be an object that brings up warm memories, such as those of your first love, whom you snuggled with and first kissed. Additionally, look at all the details of your dream and try to determine if your couch is symbolic of an analyst's "couch," such as Freud had. Old dream interpretation books offer a somewhat strange but curious meaning. They say that the couch may be symbolic of a false sense of security and that you should listen to the advice of those that love you!

Cow

In our dreams, this simple domestic animal can represent a variety of very important and deeply felt issues. In some cultures the cow is a sacred symbol, representing divine qualities of fertility, nourishment and motherhood. Consider the details in your dream and make attempts to identify the individual, (it could be you), to whom the symbolism applies. Additional characteristics to consider when interpreting a dream with cows as one of the primary symbols are passivity, docility, and general contentment with life. The cow is mostly a positive dream symbol, and superstition-based dream interpretations say that grazing cows are symbols of prosperity, contentment, and happiness. *See also:* Animals

Crab

At first glance a crab seems to be a very negative dream symbol. It could represent a "crabby" or unpleasant personality. The claws could be symbolic of a clinging and hurtful person, or a side of your own personality. There may be too much dependence, clinging and forcefulness in your life. The crab may also symbolize your inability to effectively move forward and address your own difficulties. (Remember the crab often moves sideways or backwards.) Some folklore interpretations say that the crab is an omen of poor health. However, there is a more positive interpretation for the crab in your dream. In some areas of metaphysics, the crab is a representative of the sea and the sky. It represents physical nourishment that can be obtained from the sea and also intellectual nourishment. As with all water dwelling animals, the crab could also represent something in the unconscious and the emotions. *See also:* Animals, Cancer

Crown

A crown made of gold and jewels symbolizes power, honor, and status. It could also symbolize an accomplishment or a passage into higher levels of consciousness or spiritual awareness. When interpreting this dream, pay attention to what kind of crown it is and who is wearing it. This dream may be congratulatory, (i.e., esteem for a job well done). Different types of crowns may have varying meanings; for example, Jesus had a crown of thorns and was a martyr. All crowns are circular, and in that way they bring up issues of completeness and wholeness and point to the center of personality.

Crucifix

A cross can have several seemingly varying connotations, or the interpretation may be multifaceted. It may represent your spirituality and the coming together of all different parts of your personality. It is a Christian symbol and you can think about what it means to you. The other interpretation may be less spiritual and more of a reflection of how you are feeling. A cross is a symbol of pain and suffering. Think if you are feeling as though you are being "crucified" by something that is going on in your life.

Crying

In our dreams we experience a variety of emotions. Crying in the dream state generally has the same meaning as crying in daily life. It is a release of negative emotion, frustration, or fear. On the other hand, you could be experiencing the tears of joy. Due to repression or denial, sometimes people are unable to express their feelings. In the dream state some of our defense mechanisms may relax and an emotional release occurs. Some emotional dreams may be compensatory in nature. Thus, if you never cry in daily life, you may cry in your dreams.

Dagger

Daggers, knives, and swords could represent significant feelings of anger toward yourself and others. If you kill or wound a perceived enemy in your dream, your unconscious mind may be encouraging you to conquer your fears. Freud thought that all such objects were phallic symbols.

Dancing

Dancing in your dream suggests that on some level you feel joy, happiness, and a sense of victory. If you are not in a good mood, and don't feel very joyful, this dream may be compensatory in nature. It may be trying to balance negativity and stress that you feel in daily life. Superstition-based dream interpretation says that dreaming of dancing predicts happy times ahead. Depending on the content of this dream, it may have some sexual connotations.

Danger

A dangerous situation in your dream might reflect a dangerous or threatening situation in daily life. Take the hint and pay closer attention to your finances, business matters, health, and things in general. As compensation, danger in your dream may be a positive sign and an indication that you are capable of overcoming current obstacles.

Death

Dreaming about death is very common and it can be interpreted in many different ways. Death is usually a symbol of some type of closure or end. It implies an end to one thing and a beginning of another. Death dreams usually have positive symbolism. If you are the dead person in your dream, it could imply that you would like to leave all of your worries and struggles behind and begin anew. Dreaming about someone that you care about may express your fear about losing him or her. Dreaming that one of your parents died may express fear of loss, but it also may be an unconscious valve through which you release anger and other negative feelings. In some cultures dreaming about death and dying is a very good omen that represents longevity and prosperity. *See also:* Coffin, Zombie, Smothering

Decapitation

This dream suggests that the dreamer is losing control. In a decapitation there is a dramatic and violent separation of the head from the body. Under normal circumstances the mind controls and directs the body. This dream suggests that the dreamer may be under the control of his bodily drives and may be separated from rational thoughts and feelings. Disassociation may be occurring in regard to some behavior or issue in life. However, this dream may have other meanings. This includes excessive concern about punishment and indicates that there may be severe pressure and anxiety in the dreamer's life.

Deceased Relatives

At times we dream about deceased relatives or friends simply because we miss them. These dreams may be disturbing but most likely are a form of wish fulfillment or are based on memory through which we relive old experiences. Some people believe that in dreams they meet up with the deceased on the inner planes and engage in "real" interactions with them. It is normal to miss and long for the people that we loved and that have left the physical body. Therefore, it is not surprising that they will pop up in your dreams from time to time. A personal belief system plays a large role when obtaining a satisfying interpretation for dreams in which the dead talk to the living.

Deer

As like with most other animals, the deer in your dream may represent some aspect of your intuition or it may be a message from your unconscious. In some parts of Asia, deer are considered to be conductors of soul and thus the robes of shamans are usually made out of deerskin. The Indians of North and South America also gave deer a spiritually important role. They believed that the souls of men passed into deer at the time of death. They also believed that a dying deer was a negative omen, which usually represented droughts that in turn foretold of very difficult times ahead. In the modern world, we generally see deer as gentle forest animals. Deer are characters in children's stories and Santa Claus uses them to bring gifts to all. Thus, the deer in your dream may be a symbol of gentle and helpful parts of your psyche. In order to understand the message of the dream, think about what situation in your life would benefit from gentleness and soulfulness?

Defecation

Dreams that include excretory functions usually represent cleansing and emotional release. Look at all of the details of the dream in order to obtain meaning. Ask yourself which emotions you may be releasing: anxiety, anger, mockery, annoyance, etc. Some very old folklore interpretations suggest that dreaming of feces is a good omen that suggests a financial gain. *See also:* Feces

Desert

At times a desert in a dream symbolizes the unconscious and represents the dreamer's sense of separation from it. Deserts are generally barren with little vegetation or animal life. The desert in your dreams could be bringing up issues of stagnation and periods of little growth in your life. Also, the desert could represent your loneliness and feelings of isolation. However, if you live close to the desert or love the desert, this may be a positive symbol. For some the desert may be a place where they can commune with nature and feel a sense of peace.

Devil

Dreaming about devils and demons is usually very frightening and you may awake from fear. The devil does not generally represent something outside of you. It usually symbolizes the most negative and least developed part of you. It may be that part of you that is ignorant and destructive. You can determine the meaning and message in your dream by looking at all of the details carefully. All dreams are good dreams in that they bring unconscious materials to the conscious mind. Only then can you begin to effectively cope with the more unpleasant sides of your personality. Carl Jung called this negative side the "shadow." The devils in your dreams could be representations of your personal shadow or they could be a glance at the collective shadow. *See also:* Satan

Diamond

Diamonds are valuable, timeless, and very precious. Dreaming about diamonds may have several different meanings. It could represent love and money, as well as universal truths and spiritual consciousness. The diamond is an object of desire and symbolizes those things that are most valuable to you. We are all constantly in pursuit of those things that we have not obtained but want and need in order to feel complete. Your dream may help you to decipher what is most valuable and then give you clues where to find it.

Digging

The interpretation of this behavior in a dream depends on your circumstances and on the details, which is true for most dreams. Digging is generally considered to be difficult work or hard labor. You could be "digging" around for the truth or trying to get to the bottom of things. Alternately, you could be "digging your own grave." Therefore, consider your feelings in the dream and what you were digging. Were you working a difficult area, or digging in fertile soil? *See also:* Dirt/Earth

Dinosaurs

Dinosaurs are always fascinating, sometimes lovable, mostly dangerous, and they are alive only in our imaginations.

Consider all of the details of the dream and try to tie these ideas to some aspect of your life. The dinosaur, whether you have given it a positive or negative connotation, represents something from your past or an aspect of your personality that you have altered over time. Dinosaurs may represent old issues that have not been properly addressed and that continue to have the power to affect your life in the present.

Dirt/Earth

Dreaming about dirt, as in something dirty, could represent your state of mind or a situation from your daily life. It could symbolize a relationship, a business venture, or any other part of your life where you or someone else has been less than honest and honorable. Dirt in your dreams could also represent your unwholesome attitudes and a devious state of mind. This dream, depending on its details, may be encouraging you to clean up "your act" inside and out.

Dreaming about soil and the earth usually symbolizes fertility and the potential to grow. Rich soil may be an indication that the time is right for work and new beginnings. Dreaming about dry, barren soil may be a reflection of your negative mood. It may include feelings of depression or general feelings of boredom and emptiness.

Disasters

Dreaming about natural disasters, such as earthquakes and floods, is not that uncommon. People usually have these dreams at a time of many changes in their lives. Most people have ambivalent feelings about change and some resist even positive changes. Therefore, quick shifts in life style or some type of crisis may bring about dreams of natural disasters. Please look up specific disasters by name. *See also:* Flood, Earthquake, Volcano

Disease

The word disease literally means out of ease. Before you begin to interpret this dream on a psychological or metaphysical level, first check your health. The dream could refer to physical or emotional health. *See also:* Illness

Diving

Diving in a dream suggests that you are trying to "get to the bottom" of a current situation or feeling. Water symbolizes the unconscious. Thus, another interpretation for this dream may be that you are delving into your unconscious. Finally, Freud thought that diving may have sexual connotations and represents intercourse.

Doctor

Dreaming about a doctor may represent a need for physical, emotional, or spiritual healing. Doctors are respected authority figures and we usually follow their advice and guidance in regard to our well being. Depending on your belief system, the doctor in your dream could also represent your higher self or inner guidance. If you are currently experiencing a health problem and doctors are a part of your daily/weekly life, this dream may be symbolic of real life difficulties. However, the dream is most likely based on a past event, a memory, or refers to a current need for healing, rather than a prediction of the future.

Dog

Dogs in dreams could symbolize a large variety of ideas and concepts, but mostly they are symbolic of the dreamer's defensive structure and may represent personal boundary issues. Carefully consider all of the details and the mood in your dream. First, if you have a dog, it may be natural to dream about him. We become emotionally attached to our dogs and we dream about them just as we dream about anything else that is important to us. Otherwise, dogs could symbolize loyalty and hard work. If someone calls you a dog, it is a negative reflection on your personality. If you are being treated like a dog, you are most likely being abused in some way. On the metaphysical level, dogs are considered to be the guardians of the underworld. Finally, dogs could represent the more basic or "animal" parts of our nature and some think that they specifically represent male energy.

Doll

Dolls in dreams are lifeless images of real people. They are suggestive of a person that is not genuine and does not express her feelings. Most dreams are about our personal issues and concerns and not about others. Therefore, think about yourself and try to see if you have been behaving in such ways that have been less than "real." Dolls as a dream symbol may represent the way you relate and interact with your internal and external environments. If feelings of detachment and phoniness prevail in your daily life, then they may be reflected in this dream.

Dolphin

Dolphins represent friendliness, communal living, rescue, communication, and affection. They are water dwelling mammals and in our dreams they represent our willingness and ability to navigate through emotions. They represent positive messages from our unconscious minds. Dolphins could also represent a positive connection between our consciousness and to those parts of the psyche that are a mystery and largely unconscious. *See also:* Water, Whale

Donkey

Dreaming about this interesting and amusing animal may have several different and opposing interpretations. Therefore, it is very important that you pay attention to the details and the emotional tone of the dream. A donkey may represent humility, honor, and "royalty" in disguise. On the opposite end of things, it may symbolize stubbornness and an unyielding personality. Also, it may represent a person who has many burdens and carries a "heavy load." Either way, the individual symbolized by the donkey has redeeming qualities that include ruggedness, endurance, and loyalty.

Door

Doors are passageways and in our dreams that is their symbolism. Going through a door may represent going from one state of consciousness to another or from one inner plane to another. Locked or closed doors may represent an obstacle or opportunities that are not currently available to you. Many doors may represent your current choices.

Dragon

This large, mystical creature may represent large and mystical forces inside of you. In the Far East it is believed that the dragons are spiritual creatures that navigate through the air and through the sky. In the West, dragons are considered to be dangerous creatures that need to be destroyed. As far as dream symbols go, the dragon may represent the enormous power in your unconscious. It could symbolize repressed unconscious material, including fear. However, the dragon in our dreams is generally a positive symbol. It may represent a period of time when the dreamer will confront his fears and empower himself to effectively cope with negative emotions, extreme materialism, and be able to obtain greater inner and outer freedom.

Drowning

Dreaming about drowning is common and it invokes fear. However, it may have positive significance. This dream suggests that the dreamer may be overwhelmed by unresolved emotions, old issues, or a current crisis. It suggests that a release of the old is necessary in order to emerge and begin anew. This dream serves to awaken the dreamer to embrace and to effectively cope with problems and negativity in his life.

Drugs

The interpretation of drugs in your dreams depends on the relationship you have with drugs in your daily life and whether they are doctor prescribed or not. If you are a drug user, then the drugs are an extension of what you normally do, and you need to look at the other details of your dream to get a good interpretation. However, if you use drugs rarely or never, then this dream could represent a need to get well, to escape from daily stress, and a desire to get quick relief. The drugs could be suggesting a need for healing and getting in balance. Your unconscious mind may be suggesting outrageous things in hopes that you get the message to "have fun, dream dreams, and get out of your own head!" Please keep in mind that the purpose of dreams is to raise our consciousness and to assist us in having better lives. The message in the dream about drug use is most likely not encouraging you to use drugs but it may represent a need to feel better or get better.

Duck

A duck is a very interesting bird and the message it conveys is generally positive. Ducks are well adapted to navigate and survive on land and in the water. They can swim, walk, and fly. Ducks are flexible and multi-talented. Dreaming about this bird suggests that you or someone else in your life is very flexible and can competently deal with emotional issues. Superstition-based dream interpretations say that ducks are very good omens and that you will "float" away from your current difficulty. *See also:* Animals, Birds

Dwarf

At times people will see dwarfs, midgets, or very small people in their dreams. These images seem to represent, or allude to, the childlike creative powers of the unconscious. You can think of the dwarf as a "worker" in your unconscious. He could represent some childlike condition that has the potential and power to influence your life. Consider the details and the emotional tone in the dream and make an attempt to connect it to a situation in your daily life. The dwarf suggests possibilities for learning and brings to the conscious mind messages from the unconscious.

Eagle

Carl Jung said that birds represent thoughts while birds in flight symbolize moving and changing thoughts. Birds are generally associated with freedom and abandon. In old dream interpretation books, birds are considered lucky omens. Doves and eagles are generally spiritual symbols. Your dream depends on its details, but if the birds in your dream were flying free, it may be symbolic of spiritual, psychological, or physical freedom. An eagle is a powerful bird and the unconscious message may be prosperity, success, and liberation from tedium. The eagle is also a bird of prey and some negative connotations can be made. If the eagle is on the attack or the dream is frightening, reflect on your own aggressive and predatory thoughts and tendencies.

Ear/Earring

Your unconscious mind may be suggesting a need to become more attentive to and more aware of internal and external stimuli. In order to learn we must listen to inner and outer voices. Good listening skills are a source of information that enables us to respond more appropriately to the world around us.

Earthquake

Unlike some of the other dreams about natural disasters, earthquakes usually symbolize parts of the dreamer's physical reality rather than his emotional life. The earthquake in the dream may be representing financial difficulties, health issues, or any number of other problems that could occur in daily life. An experience that is "shaking" you up, and changing your daily life, could be creeping into your dream state and showing up as an earthquake. *See also:* Disaster

Eating

To interpret this dream adequately you need to consider all of its details including what type of food you were eating, if you were eating alone, with strangers, or with familiar people. Eating usually symbolizes comfort, pleasure, and love, and most people use and misuse food on a daily basis. We nourish our bodies and stuff our feelings with food. Eating is a part of life and for some of us it is a problem. If you are on a perpetual diet and are depriving yourself of food, then this dream may be compensatory in nature. If you are feeling lonely or lack warmth, you may have dreams of eating. Eating in a dream suggests a need for physical, psychological, or spiritual nourishment.

Eggs

Eggs are symbolic of something new and fragile. They represent life and development in its earliest forms and, as such, the possibilities are limitless. At times, eggs can represent captivity or entrapment. Carl Jung said that eggs represent our captive souls. Therefore, the egg in your dream may very well represent you in the most profound sense. Are you trapped in a shell or did you break out of it and are you now free to soar?

Elephant

Elephants in dreams may represent knowledge, power, and strength. They are also associated with long memory and "thick skin." However, depending on the dream's details, the elephant may be a symbol of a large burden. Additionally, in the dream you may be making efforts to remember something important and of great magnitude.

Elevator

Going up and down in the elevator may symbolize going from one state of consciousness to another. Messages from the unconscious may be accessible. Some believe that the elevator may be a symbol of a boring and mechanical sex life. On a more pragmatic note, the elevator may simply represent the "ups and downs" of life. If you are ascending, then you may perceive your current situation as optimistic and moving upward. If you are descending, you may be experiencing some negativity and helplessness.

Envelope

Mail or letters usually come in envelopes. When we see envelopes in our dreams, we are typically dreaming about receiving news, information, or messages from someone specific or from the world at large. If you are the individual that looks forward to mail, this dream may be positive. However, if you dread the envelopes that typically hold the monthly bills, then this dream may have negative and anxiety provoking symbolism. Typically, however, dreaming about receiving letters has positive and at times spiritual connotations. You may be coming into awareness about some aspect of your life where you make new realizations and get to the "truth" of things. Some believe that seeing many unopened envelopes in your dreams may represent missed opportunities.

Ex-Boyfriend/Girlfriend

It is very common for people to dream about ex-partners. Individuals that have been an important part of our lives continue to take up a part of our mind and heart. It is impossible to very dramatically shut the person out of thoughts and feelings. Just because the relationship ends does not mean that all is finished. As we go through relationships we learn and at times pick up "battle wounds." You will continue to dream about your ex-girlfriend or boyfriend until you "let go" of them on a very important level, or until you havelearned your lessons from that relationship. Either way, dreaming about your ex-romance does not predict future involvement. It may be wish fulfillment, reliving memories, or working out old issues. Dreams are very rarely prophetic. *See also:* People

Eyes

Eyes are complex dream symbols and can be interpreted by considering the dreamer's experiences and the details in the dream (as is the case with all dream symbols). Some say that the eyes are the windows to the soul. Eyes symbolize perceptiveness, personal outlook, clairvoyance, curiosity, and knowledge. They also reveal information about personal identity and suggest to the dreamer what he should pay attention to. Closed eyes are said to represent fear and an unwillingness to see clearly. Superstition-based dream interpretations say that if the eyes in your dream are beautiful they represent peace. Crossed eyes may be an unconscious warning about someone's character, integrity, or misperceptions.

Eyeglasses

If the person in the dream normally wears eyeglasses then this symbol is an extension of daily life. However, if the person does not wear glasses, or the glasses are the focal point in the dream, several interpretations could be made. You may need to do a "reality check" or ask yourself if you are seeing the world through "rose-colored glasses." Either way, your unconscious mind may be encouraging you to make an attempt to see things more clearly.

Faces

It is very common to dream about all kinds of faces. Strange faces and familiar faces alike are frequent images in our dreams. Interpret your dream by considering the face and the general content of the dream. A stranger's face could represent different parts of your personality or psyche. You think that you are seeing a stranger but in actuality you are seeing a different part of yourself. Jung said that the stranger is a part of you that comes from the unconscious. A comic face may indicate that you have a conscious or unconscious need to mock or snub the conventional. Featureless faces suggest that you may feel unnoticed and unappreciated. On the other hand, some believe that the blank or unclear face represents a teacher. That is, someone who is there to show and teach you a lesson, but you are unprepared for it and so the face is blank. Smiling faces are representative of happy thoughts and feelings and possibly anticipation of a joyful event in the near future. Always remember the compensatory nature of dreams and their ability to point to the opposite of what you experience in daily life.

Fainting

Dreams that we remember are those that have penetrated through our ego defenses, their messages having begun to come into our conscious awareness. Often, we do not have a full understanding of the meaning of a particular dream. Awareness is a long and continual process. If you remember dreams in which you are fainting, the setting of the dream and the details leading to the fainting spell are important. Fainting in your dream suggests that you are unable to consciously confront the issue or the topic that is being raised by the unconscious. In daily life, we faint under specific conditions. For example, when we are physically ill or when environmental conditions, such as heat, powerful smells, traumatic events, or dramatic visual images, overcome us. In the dream, internal forces, images, or emotions that may be too powerful for us to process may have an overwhelming effect on the dream ego and fainting occurs. The fainting dream may be the first step in a process of becoming more aware of a particular area of your life. The unconscious will continue to send up messages and eventually you may be able to experience the unconscious psychic event that currently results in fainting.

Fairies

These mystical, magical creatures are a part of European, Roman and Greek folklore. They are known for their fickle nature, for their ability to grant wishes and for their whims of trickery. Fairies have a capacity for malice, their tools are wands and rings and they can generally be found in groups of three. The idea of three fairies is at times interpreted as representing childhood, adulthood, and old age, or birth, life, and death. Fairies may be called the "mistresses of magic" and they may symbolize the extraordinary powers of the human spirit and our fundamental capacity of imagination. Alternatively, we may want to hold on to beliefs in magical powers that will save us from ourselves. In order to be well-adjusted human beings, we need to adapt to our environment and accept our limitations. The fairy in your dream may be interpreted according to the details of the dream and according to your current issues or developmental dilemmas. Is the fairy in your dream providing hope by encouraging you to be creative and resourceful, or is she playing tricks on you and perpetuating your desire to be saved by magic?

Falling

This is a common dream which usually represents underlying fears and feelings of inadequacy and helplessness. Interpret your dream by considering your primary fears, current difficulties, and situations in your life that seem to be on a downward spiral, especially those situations that seem outside of your control (financial, romantic, etc.). Some people believe that if you keep falling in your dream and don't wake up that you will die at the point of impact. This is absolutely not true. In a falling dream you wake up out of fear and not because of danger of dying. Superstition-based dream interpretations say that if you fall a long distance in your dream and get hurt, be prepared for really hard times ahead, but if you fall and are not injured your upsets will be minor and temporary.

Famous people
See also: Actor

Father

Dreams with fathers in them can be looked at on several different levels. You may be dreaming about your father and expressing your feelings about him in a safe way. Traditionally, a father dream can be seen as symbolizing authority and power. In the dream you may be expressing your attitude about strengths and weaknesses as they relate to your position in life and your general attitude toward society. The image of the father could also represent the "collective consciousness," the traditional spirit, and the yang.

Fear

If you are experiencing great fear in your dreams, you are having nightmares. These types of dreams are positive because your unconscious mind is trying to tell you something. If you have repressed issues, they may be coming to the surface. Think about the fear in your dreams and try to be honest with yourself. Face your fears and as a great American president once said "The only thing we have to fear is fear itself." Having fearful dreams seems to be relatively common. Most dreams are unpleasant and that is the nature of our private unconscious. Issues and concerns, repressed emotions, and daily stress all contribute to an uneasy sleep and to fear-filled dreams.

Feces

Dreams containing feces may be odd but they are not uncommon. Feces represent those things that you no longer need, things that are currently garbage or waste and need to be discarded. This dream may represent healthy psychological progress. It may indicate that you are cleansing yourself of unnecessary and possibly hurtful attitudes, ideas, and emotions. At times, and depending on the details of the dream, feces could represent a contaminated area of your life, mind, or spirit. Look at the details and consider if the image of feces is in regard to something that you have been trying to clean or if it brings up stress provoking thoughts, confusion, and difficult and unresolved areas of your life. In some cultures people believe that if you are dreaming about feces you will soon prosper financially. (Feces in the dream mean money in the hand.) *See also:* Defecation

Feet
For some people, dreaming about feet can be a very sexy dream. Besides sexual connotations, the dreams can represent your ability to move forward in life. Dreams with feet in them point to how well you are balanced and grounded.

Fences
May represent your level of self-control. Maybe you need more or less of it. Additionally, this dream may express your need for privacy or connote feelings of being trapped. The details of this dream are vital to its interpretation, as is your general personality type. Are you very guarded or are you open emotionally and psychologically?

Ferris wheel
The Ferris wheel could be symbolic of the "circle of life." It may represent the ups and downs of life that create the total life experience. The circle is one of the most important dream symbols. It points to the center of personality and our being that in turn brings up issues of completeness and wholeness in our lives. Since the Ferris wheel is associated with fun and excitement, this dream may be an encouragement for the dreamer to "lighten up," see the larger picture, and possibly develop a more positive attitude.

Fighting

It usually symbolizes **anger** and confusion that comes about in times of change. If nothing is changing in your life, it may be a clue that a change is needed or that you want to change internally. Fighting with strangers usually represents an internal struggle. Fighting with familiar people may be an extension of daily life and a reflection on your relationship with them.

Fire

This is a very complex symbol that can have both negative and positive connotations. When interpreting this dream, you need to consider all of its details and your emotional responses in the dream. Fire can be a deeply spiritual symbol representing transformation and enlightenment. On the other hand, it could represent danger, anger, passion, pain, or fear. Is the fire in your dream destroying something or simply warming you? Are you currently engaging in negative behaviors or are you knowingly making wrong (or destructive) choices? Your unconscious mind may be warning you and at the same time encouraging you to alter those things in your life that may be hurtful and dangerous.

Fish

Some people believe that when you dream about fish you will soon find out that you or someone you know is pregnant (water of the womb). Others believe that if you see fish in your dreams, it is a forecast for sickness and poor health. In Christianity, Christ is at times represented by the fish symbol (spirituality). These water dwelling animals may represent messages from our unconscious and indicate to us how well we navigate through our emotional waters. They could symbolize body and soul nourishment and navigation through the unknown depths of our psyche.

Flies

These insects are annoying and they take away from the enjoyment of any moment or situation. Consider the details of your dream and try to figure out if these flies represent anything in your daily life. They could symbolize people and things that get in your way or they could mean that you are currently experiencing annoyance and frustration. Consider whether you are successfully getting rid of the flies in your dream or if they are overwhelming. This may give you a clue as to how well you are coping with distraction and frustration.

Floating

Floating in water can be symbolic of floating on top of your emotions and being in harmony with the unconscious. Floating through the air has the same symbolism as flying. Floating usually represents your current feelings of peacefulness and general freedom. On a more negative note, floating could also be symbolic of your aloofness, lack of connection, or a need to become more grounded. In order to interpret any dream appropriately, some self-evaluation and honesty is required. Meaning of dreams is very personal and specific for each dreamer.

Flood

Heavy rain and the melting of snow usually cause floods. Water in any form, including rain and snow, symbolizes emotions. Dreaming about being in a flood is an indication that the dreamer is currently experiencing powerful emotions that may be overwhelming. The flood in your dream could represent a very powerful, or even violent, emotionally cleansing experience. But don't worry, just like in an actual flood, waters recede and so do emotions. Water at times represents the flow of life and this dream may point to your feelings of being overwhelmed by it. Depending on the content of the dream and your emotional experience in it, the flood could also represent sexuality and be a sexual dream symbol. *See also:* Disasters

Flowers

When we look at flowers, most of us feel some joy and vitality. At the very least, we appreciate their beauty and see their value. Flowers are beautiful and in our dreams they could represent the simplest feelings of contentment or the deepest feelings of spiritual completeness. A circular flower is a friendly sign that could be the "mandala" symbol or the symbol of wholeness that represents the "psychic center of the personality." Additionally, the colors could symbolize the psychic centers in our bodies called chakras. Flowers also represent hope and positive growth, along with simplicity, innocence, and possibly virginity.

Flying

Dreams of flying are common and most people can recall having flown in a dream or two. There are many ideas as to what this means. Some people believe that flying in our dreams can be an actual out of body experience through which we travel to different places on this physical plane as well as into the inner planes (mostly the astral). Edgar Cayce thought that astral travel or "soul travel" might be a precursor to becoming lucid in a dream. Carl Jung's idea was that in a flying dream we are expressing our desire to break free of restrictions and limitations. We have a desire to be free and above all difficulties! Alfred Adler thought that this dream was a type of a superiority dream in which we reveal the desire to dominate and be above others. Focusing on the libido, Freud thought that flying was another way to express sexual desires. The details of your dream will give you clues as to what it symbolizes, if your dream was a spiritual experience or ego based. Enjoy it, flying is fun!

Fog

When driving, fog is an obstacle or a hindrance that makes things obscure. In a dream it may represent those things that are creating confusion and prevent the dreamer from seeing clearly. The setting of the dream may also give you clues about the area of life that it is referring to. Is the fog over water or land; are you in familiar or unfamiliar surroundings? Does the dream represent the journey into the unconscious, where things are obscure and mysterious, or does it symbolize a part of daily life that is unclear, ambivalent, and challenging? Either way, if the fog lifts before the dream ends, it suggests that awareness and clarity are forthcoming. However, if the fog in the dream was oppressive and frightening, take some time to reflect on what causes such feelings in daily life.

Food

People often dream about food. All types of food are a consistent part of a dream life. Anything from meat to elbow macaroni comes up through our unconscious and leaves

vivid memories upon awakening. Food is symbolic of a large variety of things. It could symbolize pleasure and indulgence. To the perpetual dieter, the dream could have a "compensatory" function where the food that is denied to the individual during the day shows up in the dream state. Dreams could additionally symbolize physical, mental, spiritual, and emotional nourishment.

Forest/Woods

They may represent your unconscious or your "mental space." If you are lost in the woods, it may be a reflection of feelings of confusion and lack of clear direction. The dark and threatening woods may represent the dark and unexplored areas of the psyche.

Friends

Our dreams are full of symbolism with their messengers being all different types of people. It is very common to dream about our friends. These are individual who are emotionally valuable to us and we learn about ourselves through them. Dreams are very rarely prophetic, thus whether you dream was good or bad, don't expect it to come true. This dream is more than likely attempting to bring up uncomfortable feelings that you have about yourself or others. (Remember "uncomfortable" does not necessarily mean bad.) Dream are created by our own thinking processes, our own thoughts (conscious or unconscious) create dreams; thus, the mind that created the dream also knows its meaning!!! See *also:* People.

Frog

Old dream interpretation books say that frogs are good omens and represent happiness and great friendships. From a more modern point of view, frogs may be considered symbols of the unconscious because they live in the water. Frogs also represent transformation of the positive kind.

Fruit

Fruit represents abundance and prosperity. As a result of the seeds that they carry, they may also represent new beginnings. In biblical stories, mythology, and literature in general, fruits have enjoyed much symbolic meaning. They may represent sexual desires and the search for wealth and immortality. In order to understand the meaning of the fruit in your dreams, consider your current strivings and psychological space. Also, consider whether the fruit was ripe, rotting, or bitter. All of the details will help you to understand whether you have a lustful heart, are at a new frontier, or have missed opportunities for growth and pleasure.

Funeral

Dreaming about funerals does not necessarily symbolize physical death for you or anyone else. It could instead symbolize an ending of a different kind. You may be burying relationships, conditions, or even emotions that you no longer need and that are no longer conducive to your personal growth. On the other hand, this dream may symbolize the burying of sensitivities and emotions that are too difficult to cope with. It may reflect numbness or a feeling that is the opposite of aliveness, such as depression and emptiness. Either way, burying a person that is alive

suggests some emotional turmoil. Please consider all of the details in this dream to find the appropriate message. Old dream interpretation books say that dreaming about funerals is a dream of the contrary. Instead of sadness, the dreamer will experience happiness and go to celebrations, such as weddings. *See also:* Coffin, Death

Game

People dream about all different types of games. Some are simple and borrowed from daily life, like basketball or Monopoly. Other games in dreams are bizarre, incredible, totally unrealistic, and some are even sadistic. To interpret the dream you must consider its greater context and your emotional reactions in it. Some games are simply a form of entertainment from your unconscious. You may be having fun in your dream. This is not all that common, but it does happen from time to time. Other "game" dreams may represent the challenges in your life, your competitive nature, or your childishness. They may point out goals to be achieved or are a simple way to let out steam. The game in your dream could also represent "the game of life." This is not an original thought on my part, but it deserves attention and consideration. If you are playing a strange game with people from your daily life, consider your interactions with them and the role that each individual plays.

Garage

This is an interesting symbol and many people have requested that it be added to the dictionary. Traveling is very common theme in dreams and traveling in a car is the most common. Traveling in a vehicle generally can represent our journey through life—or a portion of our life's journey. Finding yourself in a garage or a parking lot can be interpreted in several different ways. First, consider the content of your dream and your current dilemma or situation in life. The parked car could represent a period of inactivity and indecision in your life. The dream could be pointing out that you have been idle for a period of time and that it may be a good time to "get a move on." The more positive interpretation of this dream may be that the parked car is symbolic of a reflective period or mood. You may be in "park" for a while so that you can rest, relax, regroup, and think things over.

Garbage

The unconscious mind may be hinting to you that the time for "throwing out" unnecessary things is at hand. Letting go of clutter frees the mind and makes more room in the closet! The garbage in your dream could also represent those things from your past or in your life today that are not worth keeping or are literally rubbish. It has been said that "cleanliness is next to godliness," and there is something to that. Removing "garbage" from the mind, spirit, and body is not only necessary, but it is also at times accomplished in our dreams.

Garden

It may be a symbol of lost innocence or youth. Folklore tells us that dreaming of beautiful gardens is symbolic of great happiness and love. If the garden is wild, it means that you may have difficulties but with some care and attention you are capable of overcoming them.

Genitals

This typically sexual dream brings out your attitudes and concerns about your sexuality. If you are feeling guilty, stressed or concerned about your sexual activities (or a lack of them), they will be reinforced in these explicit dreams containing sexual organs. If you are dreaming about the sexual organs of other people, you may be concerned about their sexuality or other troubling issues that are surrounding them. Dreaming about sexual organs usually has something to do with sex—BUT not necessarily. Therefore think about the other details in the dream and consider issues such as personal power, fertility, and any other associations that you can make regarding the genitals from the dream.

Ghosts

Some believe that the ghosts in their dreams are real representations of the dead. This is an unlikely explanation of this dream. More likely the ghost is representing a part of you that is unclear and that you do not understand. At times, ghosts represent those things that unattainable or fleeting. Demonic types of ghost images may represent your negative tendencies, unpleasant parts of your personality, or your "shadow." Old superstition-based dream interpretations say that dreaming of friendly ghosts is a lucky omen, and that you should be receiving unexpected good luck. On the other hand, if you were very frightened by the ghost in your dream, then others will try to impose their will on you and you must be vigilant in order to stand up to it.

Gift

Giving and receive gifts is usually a pleasant occasion and both parties benefit from the exchange. Dreaming about gift giving may be a reflection on positive exchanges that are occurring in your daily life. Some say that to give and to receive is the same thing. Keep this in mind and also remember that the most valuable gifts may be emotional and spiritual in nature and that your dream may be attempting to make you aware of such gifts. Consider all of the details in the dream and make attempts to connect them to internal and personal realities or daily events.

Glass

Very important things are made out of glass. Amongst them are windows that allow sunshine into our homes, drinking glasses, seeing glasses, etc. Glass makes our lives more comfortable and we rarely, if ever give it any thought. Consider the details of your dream and try to figure out how this dream about glass is relevant to you. If glass is shattered in your dream, it could symbolize breaking of both negative and positive things. For example, it could represent the breaking of illusions, denial, and deception. On the more negative side, it could also represent the shattering of dreams or hopes that a person has been holding close to his heart. Old dream interpretation books say that looking through a clear glass is a sign of good luck and looking through a dirty glass symbolizes domestic difficulties.

Goat

When interpreting dreams with goats in them, consider the characteristics that we associate with these animals. We consider them to be sturdy and tenacious. Historically, lambs are sacrificial and when we place blame on an individual we may call him a "scapegoat." Additionally, in pagan mythology goats are considered to be symbols of sexual vitality. Look at the details of your dream and see if you can connect any of these characteristics to yourself or someone else in your daily life. *See also:* Animals

God

Regardless of whether we believe in a God or not, all of us have been exposed to the idea of a supreme and omnipresent being. The dilemma over the existence of God is probably the most common dilemma of them all. Everyone from time to time will have a dream about "God." Its symbolism depends on the dreamer. God in our dreams can be considered a positive or self-affirming symbol. It represents truth, purity, and love. It also represents the creative energy that is abundant in all of us (whether we know it or not). For a certain number of people in the dream state, God may have negative connotations. For them God could represent eternal punishment and damnation, and invoke massive amount guilt. Most religions consider dreams to be a pathway to God or to the spiritual realm. Through dreams we have an opportunity to have experiences that are not available during the day. *See also:* Jesus

Gold

Dreaming about gold could be a reflection of concerns that you have about your most precious valuables or a reference to "alchemist's gold" which is usually spiritual in nature. If you are losing gold in your dream, it may express your anxieties over a missed opportunity. However, remember, "All that glitters is not gold." Your unconscious mind may be reminding you not to judge things on appearances alone.

Grave/Graveyard

Graves are generally depressing and represent some form of death. On a very physical level this dream does not appear to be a very happy omen. However, the dream could also have deeper and more spiritual meaning. It could represent things that require deep thinking and are not "on the surface." Graves could also symbolize the unconscious. If someone close to you has recently died, it may be normal for you to have dreams about graveyards and death. However, if this dream is coming up and there has been no death in the family, consider your feelings in daily life. If you are feeling depressed or helpless in any way, "look inside" and make attempts to increase your self-awareness and your spiritual identity.

Guns

The gun in your dream could represent several different things, so please pay attention to the details and to the mood of the dream. The gun could symbolize the male sex organ, aggression, harshness, and fear. This dream may have several connotations, or your unconscious mind may be telling you not to harbor your negative feelings but to express them more freely before they become explosive. On the more positive side of things, the gun could simply represent your need to protect yourself either emotionally or physically or both. If the gun in the dream is used to hurt or kill you or someone else, please consider your current difficulties, hostile feelings or serious arguments, which you may have within yourself or with others. *See also:* Shooting, Blood

Hair

Hair is highly valued by most cultures. It is a symbol of vanity, security, sensuality, sexual appeal, and of youth. In some cultures women are not allowed to show their hair outside their homes. Wealthy men go through painful surgery and spend thousands of dollars to replace lost hair follicles. Needless to say, hair is a valuable dream symbol. It represents physical and spiritual strength. Samson's hair was the source of his strength and virility. In our dreams hair can represent our thoughts, knowledge, and reasoning. White or gray hair represents age and wisdom while body hair may symbolize protection and warmth. When interpreting a dream make attempts to identify a primary issue and connect it to a situation in your daily life. *See also:* Beard

Hands

We express ourselves with our hands, and appropriate reading of body language is a valuable source of information. Likewise, in the dream state the hands may reveal information about emotions, intentions, and overt behaviors. For example, if in your dream you see clenched fists you may have much repressed anger. Sometimes extended hands suggest a need to develop close friendships. If the hands in your dreams are stroking you, you may be feeling sexy.

Happiness

If you are currently experiencing sadness this dream may be an attempt to compensate and to comfort you. Traditionally this may be called a dream of the contrary. Extreme happiness in a dream calls for an evaluation of daily reality in an attempt to identify those things that are difficult and painful, (i.e., things that make you feel the opposite of happy). Dreaming of happy children is said to be a good omen probably because children represent endless possibilities and opportunities for growth and development.

Hats

Hats are usually symbolic of power and authority. They also stereotype the person who is wearing it. Look at the details in your dream and notice especially who is wearing the hat. The type and quality of the hat usually represents the degree of authority and respect that your unconscious mind is giving to the person wearing it. Generally the person wearing the hat is representing a part of you. What is the hat saying about your position in life and your attitude toward it?

Heaven

Heaven represents all of those things for which most people hope. Some of us may not be convinced of its existence, but all of us have definite ideas about what heaven should be like. In your dreams it may symbolize happiness, peace, understanding, rest, love, union between God and man, and many more positive things. Some people work for a "heaven on Earth." Others believe that there are many different heavens and in their dreams they visit those places through soul travel. Whatever your belief system or your dream experience may be, this dream usually leaves you feeling positive and energized.

Hide

In daily life we hide from things that we don't want to deal with or we hide from danger. As children we played the game of "hide and go seek," while as adults we enjoy "chase and discovery." The emotional tone of your dream will reveal its meaning. If you are hiding out of danger, then you should consider those things in your life that propose a threat to you. They could be internal forces or environmental conditions. Generally, we attempt to hide our own negativity and mistakes. This dream may call for an honest reflection on personal characteristics and an evaluation of how much fear influences our lives and decision-making.

Hole

Holes, as all other dream symbols, can only be appropriately interpreted by considering the details and the emotional content of the dream. Holes in socks, clothing, furniture, etc., may represent feelings of faultiness or depravation. You may be bringing your attention to the fact that there is something missing or in need of repair in your life. At times holes can represent the female sex organs. Dark holes can symbolize the great "unknown" or the entrance to the unconscious. If there are many negative or frightening feelings associated with this dream, you may be becoming aware of some problematic or troublesome situation in your life.

Homosexuality

Sex in many different forms is frequently the topic of dreams. Sexual dreams don't always have sexual meaning. They are at times about power, control, identity, and other non-sexual issues of life. If you are homosexual, dreams regarding this particular sexual orientation are not atypical. They are simply the extension of your thoughts and feelings in the form that is the most familiar and meaningful to you. If a heterosexual person is having a homosexual dream, it may have a variety of connotations. The interpretation of this dream, as with all others, is very personal and generalizations are difficult to make. This dream may be about loving yourself, especially if the other individual in your dream is a stranger. The dream may be about integrating ideas and attitudes, and in a few rare cases may be about sexual orientation. *See also:* Sex, Intercourse

Honey

Sweet experiences and good health are in your subconscious and most likely in your life.

Horse

The horse is a noble and powerful animal. As a dream symbol it can represent a wide range of positive thoughts and ideas about self or others. Depending on the details of the dream, horses can symbolize freedom, power, and sexual energy. At times, they can also be considered messengers, relaying information from the unconscious to the conscious, from the spiritual to the physical. If you are horseback riding it suggests that you are self-assured and feel a sense of control in your daily life. Old dream interpretation books say that the color of the horse is also significant. (Remember that this is based on superstition.) Black horses are said to point out delays; white horses reinforce the positive and transformative aspects of life; gray horses may point to the difficulties in the dreamer's current situation; piebald horses are symbolic of confusion; brown horses are associated with mental pursuits; tan horses are said to be symbolic of love and sex.

Hospital

Many people reported having dreams about hospitals and surgery. This appears to be a relatively common dream setting. Most of us are in some need of healing. The healing may be physical, psychological, emotional, or spiritual. By paying attention to this dream you may be able to identify the source of your pain, and where and how the healing needs to take place. Think about why you or someone else was in the hospital in the dream. You may ask yourself, "What is going on in the dream? What is the prognosis, and what is the cure?" Answering these questions in light of a situation or issue from your daily life could be very helpful and, at times, enlightening. Therefore, try not to get upset by your dream, but rather pay attention to its message. Superstition-based dream interpretations suggest that if you are visiting a patient you will be receiving surprising news (good or bad), but if you are the patient, you may be currently overwhelmed by life and should ask others for help. *See also:* Pain

Hostage

Dreaming about being a hostage suggests that you may experience feelings of victimization or entrapment. This can be indicative of a situation in daily life, such as an oppressive and unsatisfactory relationship or financial difficulties. The dream suggests that you may experience feelings of powerlessness and cannot see you way out of a difficult situation. Because a hostage is taken against his will, you may be feeling as though you have been trapped by another or by circumstances. Also, the hostage situation in your dream may represent a part of your personality that is not being expressed. It could be your creativity, intellect, or inner freedom. The purpose of this dream may be to make you more aware of the limiting conditions in your life. Additionally, the dream may trigger your imagination and problem-solving abilities enabling you to see new possibilities.

Hotel

All dwelling places generally represent the dreamer's psychological, emotional, or spiritual condition. The dream may reflect a current reality, issue, or dilemma and attempt to bring the dreamer into greater self-awareness. Because a hotel is a transitory dwelling, it suggests a time away from one's responsibilities or routine. As a dream symbol it could reflect a need for rest and reflection. Depending on the details of the dream, specific information can be ascertained. For example, if the hotel is luxurious it suggests prosperity and positive decision-making. However, if the hotel is rundown and inadequate, it may reflect a time of uneasiness and depravation. Whether the hotel in your dream represented a retreat or escapism is for you to determine by examining your current daily reality. Finally, a hotel may refer to a temporary stage in life or be a form of compensation with which the dreamer eases the anxiety and stress experienced during the day.

House

It is common to dream about houses. They usually symbolize our emotional and psychological selves. All of your experiences, stages of development, and parts of your conscious and unconscious life may be represented by that house. The house may be representing issues concerning a particular dilemma in your life, or it may be more general and comprehensive. Either way, if you pay attention to the details in this dream, you may learn a thing or two about yourself. *See also:* Kitchen, Bathroom, Attic

Hug

A hug is a very pleasant dream symbol. It suggests love and tenderness. It is also symbolic of comfort and protection. Look at all of the details in your dream and look for the positive meaning. The only time that this dream symbol has negative connotations is if you were to hug or be hugged by a very negative person or something that you consider "evil." Otherwise, it is a sweet and comforting dream symbol.

Hurricane

Dreaming about hurricanes usually suggests that the dreamer is going through sudden and unpleasant changes in his life. It indicates that there is an emotional storm in the dreamer's life or on the horizon. Old dream interpretation books consider hurricane dreams to be dreams of warning and recommend that the dreamer does not take any unnecessary risks. Additionally, if you are uncertain about doing something, don't do anything at all! *See also:* Disasters

Ice

Ice, or water in the solid form, is associated with the emotions and the unconscious. Dreaming about ice suggests that you may have some emotions or denied psychological issues that are not readily accessible to you. These feelings may be negative (i.e., fear and anxiety about death or sexual frigidity). Things that are frozen are generally not usable and they do not change or grow. This dream may be pointing to feelings or thoughts that are inaccessible to you or to that part of you that is inaccessible to others. Superstition based dream interpretation books tell us that sitting on ice in your dreams is a *dream of the contrary*. It indicates that you may have a life of comfort and prosperity (this is may be silly to some but others like to hear these type of interpretations!).

Ice Cream

Eating, making, selling, or serving ice cream suggests that you are feeling contentment and satisfaction in your life. Things are well and the best is yet to come. Alternatively, you may be compensating in a dream for a lack in daily life. For example, not enough "sweetness" or sincerity during the day may bring images of ice cream into the night.

Ice-Skating

Please read the interpretation of ice and take it one step further. This dream suggests that you may have a part of your emotional or psychological life in a stagnant or inaccessible form. You may be functioning in your daily life without regard to large issues that you are denying. This is a good dream symbol that encourages you to look at those parts of your life that you are most reluctant to address but are very important to your happiness.

Illness

If you are ill in your dream, please pay attention to your health. At times our unconscious gives us warnings before we are consciously aware of any symptoms. Emotional health can also be included in such dreams, so take care of your relationships and express your feelings in positive ways. If someone you care about is ill in your dream, maybe you are concerned about losing the support and love of that person.

Incest

This could be an extremely disturbing dream, but it does not necessarily have anything to do with sex. It is possible that you may be worried about other aspects of your family life. If this dream persists, you may consider talking to a professional about it. If you are currently making important decisions, don't do anything that is morally questionable because you are already experiencing disturbing dreams associated with taboos that bring up feelings of guilt and shame.

Infidelity

Dreaming about being unfaithful suggests that you take a better look at your current relationship. What was the person in your dream giving you (emotionally or otherwise) that your real life partner does not? Communicate effectively and begin to develop those areas of your relationship that most need improvement. Understanding this dream may assist you in understanding your relationship and the level of attachment to your partner. Many people write about "dreams of cheating." Either they are cheating, or they believe that their partners are cheating on them. In either case, they are upset and outraged by such dreams. It seems logical that these types of dreams are connected to feelings of inadequacy or dissatisfaction.

Insects

Some dream interpretation books name specific insect symbols. However, the main idea to consider when you are interpreting this dream symbol is that you may currently be annoyed or "bugged" by a person or a situation in life. Use common sense and some general impressions about the specific insect when interpreting your dream. For example, if you are dreaming about bees stinging you, think about some of your relationships. If you are dreaming about ants consider you social interactions and work ethic.

Intercourse

It is very difficult to name just a few possible interpretations for this dream. It is complex and complicated, and the interpretations vary with each dreamer and with the situations in the dream. A sexual dream may be about physical pleasure but it may also be about power, control, manipulation, virility, and effectiveness. It may be a form of wish fulfillment or a memory. In most cases it is not a prediction of things to come in the near future. Freud believed that experiencing sexual pleasure in your dreams usually expresses desire, and the dream is a form of wish fulfillment. If you are watching other people having sex it may be a reflection on your emotional and mental concerns about sexual performance or interaction.

Intruder

Seeing an intruder breaking into your house or hurting you or someone else can be a very frightening dream. Depending on the level of fear this dream is, at times, a nightmare. The intruder breaking the law or breaking into your house may be a representation of an unconscious part of your psyche. Carl Jung called the negative forces the "shadow." The intruder may be a symbol of your guilt and self-indulgent attitudes or behaviors. On the other hand, it may represent the more negative side of your nature. If you had a fearful real-life experience with an intruder through this dream you may be reliving that experience and hopefully letting go of the fear.

Iris

An iris is a spring flower that symbolizes several very positive and uplifting conditions. In Japan, it is believed that the iris has the power to purify the body and protect the household from disease and evil. Iris is also a God in Greek mythology. She is a messenger who represents the link between heaven and earth and between gods and men. This is a very interesting and specific dream symbol. In order to figure out what it means to you personally, consider your current needs. Do you have a need for purification and safety or are you looking for inspiration?

Island

Dreaming about being on an island can have several different meanings and could be very revealing. Consider your mood in this dream. Was the island a place of rest, peace, or solitude? If the answer is yes, it suggests that you may need time to yourself for restoration and renewal. The sea or the ocean generally symbolizes our unconscious. Thus, if you were very lonely or fearful of the waters around you, it may be an indication that you are unwilling to look deeply into yourself. You may be afraid of the materials that are under the surface of your conscious thoughts and feelings.

Jail

Dreaming about jail may make you think that you have done something immoral or illegal, or committed an act that merits punishment. You may also have a fear of being trapped emotionally or physically. If you are the jailer, you may have an unconscious desire to exert control over others or in a particular situation. Either way, this dream suggests that you have obstacles in your life that may not be easy to overcome.

Jealousy

Experiencing jealousy in your daily life may cause you to dream about it. If you are not aware of your jealousy, your unconscious may be giving you some hints of awareness. Jealousy is usually a result of insecurity. Consider this dream a learning experience. Analyze some of your feelings of insecurity or inadequacy and then begin to deal with those issues.

Jesus

Jesus is usually a very powerful dream symbol. If you are a Christian, then you have an entire reservoir of knowledge about Him. At the most general level, Jesus is a symbol of divinity, perfection, forgiveness, and love. If you met and interacted with Christ in your dream, you may be on a search for your spiritual home. If you are dreaming about the crucifixion, you may be experiencing strong but unwarranted feelings of guilt, or an underlying fear of being persecuted without cause. *See also:* God, Cross

Jewelry

The meaning of this dream depends on your current concerns. Jewelry is usually a representation of materialistic values. Gender differences imply that for a man this dream symbolizes material wealth and for a woman, love. Careful analysis requires answering the following questions: What type of jewelry it is? Is it genuine or costume? How did you react to it and in what way was it important in the dream?

Journey

Dreaming about traveling in vehicles is very common. It represents our path in life or a part of our life's journey and it may reflect some of our fear and anticipation. For details, look up the particular vehicle. See Car, Boat, Airplane, Travel

Jungle

The jungle could represent your confusing and overwhelming thoughts regarding daily life. If you dream you are in an impenetrable jungle, your unconscious may be revealing to you the anxiety you have about a particular situation, a current difficulty, or the future. If you find yourself freely exploring the jungle, it is a positive dream image which might be encouraging you to go on a new adventure and discover unexplored areas of your own psyche. *See also:* Forest/Woods

Jupiter (Zeus)

The Greek god Zeus and the Roman god Jupiter are one and the same. Zeus is the god of gods. He is the creator of day, thunder and lightning, and the seasons, and is the "sky god." Zeus holds supreme power and his decisions are not questioned, as he is the father of gods and men. He represents external order and authority. His wisdom, power, and sense of fairness support the structure of the ancient Greek and Roman universe. Jupiter, or Zeus, is a "good father" who provides the opportunity for growth, development, prosperity, and health. Jupiter, as a planet, has a central position among the other planets in the solar system. Mercury, Venus, Earth, and Mars are on one side and Saturn, Uranus, Neptune, and Pluto on the other. Astrologically, Jupiter represents balance, organization, abundance, and optimism. If you are down on your luck or a bit disorganized, this dream may be calling for awareness of supportive internal and external forces. Our dreams often compensate for what is lacking in daily life. In this way, dreams attempt to balance the psyche. Thus, dreaming of Jupiter is reassuring and invites the dreamer to access the power in his own psyche and to embrace a positive attitude. Jupiter is a reminder that there is an order to the universe that provides us with an opportunity to have a prosperous, balanced, and joyful life.

Kangaroo

Depending on the details of the dream, dreaming about this interesting animal may have several different connotations. The kangaroo is a strong and powerful animal. It has huge feet that it uses for mobility and self-protection. Your dream may have to do with issues of strength, freedom to move, and grounding. Additionally, since we are all intrigued with a kangaroo's parenting style, this dream may be bringing up issues regarding your mother or your mothering. Superstition-based dream interpretation books say that seeing a kangaroo in your dreams foretells unexpected and exciting trips. *See also:* Animals

Key

As with most dreams, look for the obvious connections by comparing the details or the theme of your dream to your daily life. Are you trying to figure something out and "unlock" a puzzling question? Do you wish to hide something? Are you locking something up or are you opening the door? Last, but not least, does this dream have any sexual connotations?

Kidnapping

The main theme in abduction dreams is fear. The dreamer may be afraid of losing a very important part of himself or of losing his safest and most familiar surroundings. Also, the dreamer may be afraid of leaving his home, childhood, familiar support group, or long-standing ideas. These types of dreams may be most prevalent during times of psychological or physical transition and during stressful times of life when the future is somewhat uncertain. Consider the details of your dream and try to isolate and identify the fear that created the dream.

Killing

If you are killing someone in your dreams, you are probably expressing hostile feelings. Consider this an opportunity to look at your negative feelings and decide what would be the best and the least destructive way to address them. If you are a witness to a killing, you may be reflecting on changes going on around you that you don't particularly like. *See also:* Blood, Attack, Anger, Shooting

King

In African folklore, the king is said to be "the one who holds all life, human and cosmic, in his hands; the keystone of society and the universe." In the modern world, we may not associate the king with ultimate power, knowledge, or wisdom. However, historically the mythical King was highly spiritual, was the center of the wheel of life and was said to have a regulatory function in the cosmos. Psychologically, the king and the queen are said to be the "archetypes of human perfection." As a dream symbol, you can understand the king or queen in your dream by realizing that they represent your ability to achieve independence, self-understanding, and self-determination. They also represent inner wealth that will enable you to be your best and help you to reach your goals. Consciously, you may never have the desire to be a king or queen, but psychologically, these figures are symbolic of our highest potential and our desire to be the "king or queen" of our own world and our own lives. On rare occasions and depending on the details of the dream, the king and queen may represent a powerful force that is unkind and tyrannical.

Kiss

In this dream you may be expressing feelings that are difficult to express during the day. Kissing is usually an indication of warmth, affection, and happiness. If you don't receive enough love and affection in your daily life, then this could be a compensatory dream, where the dreamer is comforting himself. If you are kissing the object of your affection, the dream could be a form of wish fulfillment. Superstition-based interpretations say that if you are kissing strangers, you may have a need to conquer. If the kissing is insincere, you are pretentious, while if you see your partner kissing someone else, you may be afraid of infidelity.

Kitchen

Houses in dreams generally represent the dreamer (dreamer = house). The kitchen is the heart of the house. For most families, the kitchen is a place of warmth and nourishment (emotional as well as physical). Examine the conditions of your dream kitchen and you may become aware of some emotional needs and feelings toward yourself and others. *See also:* House

Kite

The message that is coming up from your unconscious mind may be one of renewed freedom or an accomplishment of a goal. Kites are generally associated with sweet childhood memories and a sense of abandonment in joy. If your daily life is difficult, this dream may be a form of compensation, or it may be a positive anticipation of things to come.

Knife

This tool does not have positive connotations. It may reflect the unrest and difficulty that you are experiencing. If you are self-mutilating, consider your actions and/or addictions. Take a hint from your unconscious and modify or discontinue your harmful thoughts or actions. *See also:* Killing, Dagger

Ladder

Ascension or descension on a ladder may be an unconscious reflection of your movement toward a goal. Ascending is generally a more positive symbol than descending. The ladder is suggestive of hard work and exertion of energy. The ladder may also be symbolic of the "way to heaven." You can decide whether the heaven is here on earth or in the forever after! Missing rungs may symbolize missing elements or hardships and handicaps that you could be (or are) encountering on your ascent to better and bigger things. *See also:* Stairs, Climbing

Lake

All bodies of water generally represent our emotions and our unconscious. Old dream interpretation books say that lakes are associated with romantic feelings. If the lake is calm, your love life is probably in such good shape that you feel safe. Stormy water means to strap yourself in and get ready for a bumpy ride. If you see a monster in the water, your unconscious may be suggesting that you have competition (or some unseen issue or problem). For a more serious and contemplative definition of this dream symbol, please see: Water, Ocean

Lamb

To interpret this dream most accurately, please consider all of the details in the dream and its mood. The lamb in your dream could have negative or positive connotations and it could reflect some of your personal characteristics or attributes. On the positive end, the lamb symbolizes gentleness, warmth, love, innocence, and for the spiritually minded, the Lamb of God. More negative interpretations of this dream symbol would be that the lamb in your dream is a "sacrificial" lamb, or "lamb going to the slaughter." *See also:* Animals

Lateness

If you are arriving late, your unconscious may be telling you to be more perceptive and to use more foresight when making plans. Lateness suggests that the dreamer may be feeling unprepared and distracted in a particular situation in daily life or in regard to long-term goals.

Leak

Whether it is a leaky pipe or a bottle of soda, any type of a leak is usually a waste of energy and resources. If you are dreaming about leaks, you may want to consider where you are wasting energy and resources (be it in your daily life, emotional life or thinking). Additionally, look carefully at the entire dream and see if information is being "leaked" from the unconscious to the conscious. The leaking water may represent emotions, thoughts, or insights entering slowly into the conscious experience of the dreamer.

Leech

Leeches are parasites that drain your energy and your resources. They are literally "bloodsuckers" and what they represent from your life is up to you to determine. Think about all of the draining things around you or inside of you. Usually dreams are designed to make us more aware of ourselves. Thus, the leeches may represent your own habits, thoughts, and negative emotions rather than someone in your environment. In the old days (and maybe in some remote parts of the world this is still happening) leeches were used frequently for medical purposes. They were harvested and used in case of infection, when a poisonous or harmful substance needed to be removed from the body. Maybe the leeches in your dream are there to suck out all of the negativity that you acquire throughout your day or in a particular situation.

Letter

Dreaming about receiving letters, just as in daily life, usually represents receiving news, information, or messages from someone specific, from your unconscious, or from the world at large. If you look forward to mail, this dream may have positive connotations for you. However, if you dread the envelopes that hold the monthly bills, then this dream may have negative and anxiety-provoking meaning. Typically, however, dreaming about receiving letters has positive and, at times, spiritual connotations. You may be coming into greater awareness about some aspect of your life, having new realizations, increasing your self-understanding, or getting to the truth of things that concern you. Some believe that seeing many unopened letters in your dreams may represent missed opportunities.

Library

You may be trying to assimilate some new information or idea. A library is a place of learning and is generally a good dream image. It suggests that you may be close to solving a problem or discovering something new and exciting.

Light

Whether you are dreaming or awake, light is a very positive symbol. It represents enlightenment, lifting of shadow, the acquisition of understanding and knowledge, and a positive force. Depending on the details of the dream, you may give the light spiritual or physical meaning. For some, the light may represent a higher force or power, God's presence, or rays of His love and peace. Others may find this dream reassuring as it may represent a well-lit journey through life, or simply a solution to a current problem. Light always refers to consciousness.

Lightning

Lightning represents energy and a fantastic, altering force. It is generally a positive dream symbol that represents the dreamer's "awakened" state of consciousness. At times, a sudden shift in awareness, or unpredictable news, may shock us and leave us feeling anxious. However, enlightenment of any kind has long-term positive implications. When interpreting this dream, make attempts to connect it to important and highly charged events from your daily life that have suddenly occurred or come into your awareness. *See also:* Storm

Lion

Carl Jung said that all wild animals indicate latent affects (feelings and emotions that we do not readily deal with). They are also symbolic of dangers (hurtful and negative things) being "swallowed" by the unconscious. The lion is a symbol of social distinction and leadership. The interpretation depends on the circumstances and the interactions with the lion. *See also:* Animals, Cat

Lips

In pop culture, lips are usually symbols of sexuality and sensuality. They are also symbols of communication. Old dream interpretation books say that if you see beautiful lips in your dreams, expect happy events to occur, but if you see ugly or deformed lips, look out for trouble! Who knows?

Lock

If things are locked up and we don't have the key, then it is impossible for us to get to them. Consider the details in your dream and try to decipher the message. Are you the one who is locked up inside, or are opportunities closed to you? Locks in your dreams may represent those things that are currently inaccessible to you. Other interpretations suggest that locks are symbols of security and, at times, may have sexual connotations.

Love

For some of us, love is a full-time obsession. We are concerned about the love of our parents, children, coworkers, friends, and many, many others. There is nothing more important to our emotional, psychological, or spiritual well

being than love. It is a vital part of any growth process. We need to have a healthy dose of self-love so that we can, in turn, love the world. Dreams may be filled with images of love, friendship, compassion, and lust. In the end, it is all about acceptance and belonging. To be loved is to feel accepted and have a sense of belonging. In our dreams we may be trying to figure out this mystery called love. The dream may be wish fulfilling or compensatory in nature. It may be spiritual or practical, but always deals with a significant part of our psyche or our daily lives.

M

Man

All different kinds of people clutter our dream landscape. The men in your dream may include family members or total strangers. You may dream about your father, son, husband, or friend and should interpret the dream according to its details. A man, particularly the father figure, may represent collective consciousness and the traditional human spirit. He is the yang, and his energy, when mobilized, creates the earthly realities. Depending on the details of the dream, the masculine figure could be interpreted as the Creator or Destroyer. At times, women dream about men who are strangers to them. These men may represent the women's unconscious psychic energy. Carl Jung called the stranger in a woman's dream the "animus." He represents autonomous, unconscious energy and he plays a vital role in obtaining a deeper understanding of self. At times, a strange and ominous man in men's dreams could represent their "shadow" or their negativity and darker sides of personality. *See also:* People, Women

Map

The interpretation depends on whether you are following a map to a particular destination and you feel good about it, or whether you are trying to follow a confusing chart. A confusing chart may indicate that you lack a clear sense of direction in your everyday life or are in the midst of chang-

ing long term plans. Following a good map in your dreams suggest that you are feeling confident in your current path and pursuits.

Marriage

It is a symbol of commitment and, depending on the details of your dream, you may be currently dealing with this issue. The commitment could be to your work, to yourself or to your partner. Mostly, a marriage in your dream represents the coming together all various parts of yourself, (feminine and masculine, or spiritual and rational). It could represent a greater level of awareness whereby the dreamer's conscious and unconscious elements are becoming more familiar and are embracing one another. On a more practical level, if you are not married but would like to be, this dream could also be a form of wish-fulfillment.

Mars (Ares)

The "fiery" planet is named after the Greek god Ares and Roman god Mars. He was the god of war, spring and youth. Mars was the guardian of young men and was himself highly impetuous. Mars represents energy, aggression, violence, desire, and the male sexual organs. He is sometimes the symbol of life and death. In mythology, Ares was often beaten and humiliated by his enemies. He was like an ill-tempered child who was unable to receive the amount of credit that he desired. Thus, seeing this planet in your dreams may be symbolic of your own frustrations that lead to aggressive thoughts and feelings. Mars is a symbol of male energy. This energy, when used in positive ways, creates permanent change and transformation. This dream might be encouraging you to get in touch with raw emotions and desires, to ponder upon them, and then to use them to transcend difficulties.

Masks

Masks may represent our persona and how we appear to others, the roles that we play in life such as parent, student, or worker. On the other hand, masks can be a symbol of pretentiousness. If you are wearing a mask, look inside and check if you are being sincere in your presentations, or if you are hiding something and pretending to be something you are not. If other people are wearing masks, it suggests that you may be concerned about their genuineness.

Maze

The maze could represent your current mental outlook. A maze is a frightening and confusing place. If in your dream you are trapped in a maze and are having difficulty getting to the end, then you need to stop and consider your current emotional and psychological status. I don't mean to suggest anything is terribly wrong. Simply speaking, are you often confused and unsure of which way to go? If you are facing many hard decisions this dream is a good indicator that you need to step back and look at the entire picture. Edgar Cayce said that being in a maze in a dream might be symbolic of an "emotionally disorganized" person. At times we are all emotionally disorganized and confused, but admitting this dream's message is a step in the right direction.

Medicine

Taking medication is always indicative of an attempt to restore one's health. Your unconscious mind may be encouraging you to take measures to insure your health and happiness. Consider all of the details of your dream and decide if the medication taken was helpful or hurtful. Try to connect these thoughts to your situations in daily life. *See also:* Drugs

Melody/Song

Hearing sounds in your dreams can be looked at from a spiritual point of view. Nice sounds are usually positive symbols. Some may say that in your dream state you have traveled to other higher and more spiritual plains. Traditional interpretations tell us that if you hear a familiar melody, you may bump into old friends. Psychologically speaking, you may have heard a song during the day and in your dream state you are simply replaying it. However, since dreams always have meaning, the song that you are dreaming about may have messages in it that will assist you in solving a problem or will help you to feel better.

Menstruation

It is a common dream for women and its interpretation is mostly positive. Dreaming about having your menses can be symbolic of releasing tension and worry. Women are often concerned about their reproductive system. (i.e., pregnancy, sexual relationships or their body's "time clock"). Parallel to the menstrual cycle there is a monthly emotional cycle that most women are aware of and experience. During the time of menstruation there is a release of anxiety and an attainment of emotional balance. As a dream symbol it suggests that some difficult times may be over for you and that you can relax. On occasion this dream suggests a loss of energy and disappointment.

Mercury (Hermes)

As a metal, mercury is a universal alchemical symbol representing the yin. It is the symbol of the passive and the undifferentiated state that may be found deep within the psyche. The Chinese refer to it as "liquid silver," and it corresponds to the dragon and to the bodily fluids of blood, semen, and water and, at times, to the kidneys. The planet Mercury may be seen as following the Sun (universal father; consciousness; life) and the Moon (universal mother; birth; unconscious). In Greek mythology, Hermes was the messenger of the gods and the god of speed. This intelligent and quick-witted immortal easily traveled between heaven, earth, and the underworld. Seeing the planet Mercury or the metal in your dream may represent your need for communication, adaptation, and movement. All of these may be necessary for daily life. However, this powerful dream symbol may be calling your attention to more personal and intrinsic matters. It may suggest a need to look carefully into your internal world. By doing so, you may become aware of a need to develop a more fluid ability to navigate within your psyche, which includes your thoughts, motives, feelings, and intuition; then notice the way all of these components are translated into and effect daily life.

Milk

Milk is a symbol of leaning, knowledge, plenty, fertility, and immortality. Milk as a symbol of immortality may be found in different cultures and literature, including in India, in Greek mythology, in Celtic writings, in Islam and Christianity. In his recordings, Ibn Omar wrote that Muhammad said "to dream of milk is to dream of learning or knowledge." Dreaming of milk is a very positive message from your unconscious. It may suggest that you are in need of the deepest and most fundamental type of nourishment and that it is available to you. You unconscious may be suggesting that it is time for you to grow and to learn and that it is possible for you to do that at the current time. The interpretation of dreaming about milk can also be looked at from a very different viewpoint. Milk can be a safe representation of semen and you may have unconscious (or conscious) desires for sexual relations. However, in my opinion it is unlikely that milk in dreams represents sexuality. Finally, milk is a lunar symbol and as such it is feminine. It suggests a renewal in spirit and thought, just like springtime is the renewal of nature.

Mirror

It is a symbol of vanity and superficiality. You may be concerned about your image and the way you present yourself to the world. Some say that if you see a clear image, you may be getting a glimpse of your true self. Broken mirrors always seem to be a sign of bad luck, or, at least, represent some distortions. On a deeper level the mirror can be considered to be a representation of the intellect. The intellect is an instrument of navigation and is constantly persuading us to identify ourselves. When we think about this, it makes a lot of sense. Our self-identity is very much connected to the way we look (not only superficially but also characteristically as man or woman, young or old, etc.). We use this self-identity, which is greatly a production of our intellect, to navigate through life.

Money

The significance money has in your waking life is reflected in your dream state. Money is a symbol of power and wealth. We often judge ourselves based on our ability to make it, save it, and spend it. First, consider your own relationship with money and your current financial situation, as this dream could be simple wish fulfillment. As always, consider all of the accompanying details in your dream, because they will help you to understand where your issues lie. Traditional dream interpretations indicate that losing money in your dream is a good omen, and that probably the opposite will happen. Generally, money may represent those things that are most valuable to you and not necessarily cash.

Monkey

The monkey is a symbol that needs to be understood by considering the various associations that we make when thinking about them. Monkeys may represent lust, self-satisfaction, and trickery. A monkey may also represent positive attributes, such as agility, inspiration, a sense of freedom, and a capacity to imitate. In Japan, toys that look like monkeys are given to children because monkeys are supposed to be able to drive out evil spirits. In India, the monkey is a symbol of soul. Thus, monkeys as symbols appear to have a twin meaning. Whether positive or negative, the monkey is revealing something to you about what is going on in your inner world. People usually think that monkeys are far less evolved and the expression "stop monkeying around" is understood by all. The dream with a monkey may be an encouragement from you unconscious to continue to develop your personality by staying close to your own nature.

Monster

Dreaming about monsters and demons is very common. They may represent negative forces inside of yourself and in your life. Most of the monsters are representing your own negative characteristics and tendencies. The monster in your dreams could be your fear, bad temper, negativity, smoking habit, or anything else that is hurtful and needs to be changed. The way that you deal with the monster in your dream is generally symbolic of the way you are dealing with the corresponding negativity in your daily life. If you wake up from this dream and are very frightened, just remember that your mind created those images and that their purpose is to teach you something about yourself.

Moon

The moon is an interesting symbol that connotes feminine energy; it is associated with the irrational and the intuitive. The moon affects the ocean tides, and it has been linked to madness or lunacy. Moon as a dream symbol can represent all of these things and more. As always, pay attention to the details in the dream before making conclusions. The moon could represent romance and our earthly impulses and passions. It could reveal things about the nature of soul and the unconscious. For those lucky people, the moon can reflect their inner peace and feelings of serenity and security.

Morning

When you are interpreting a dream, the setting is generally important. It provides clues about the larger and the true meaning of the dream. The morning is a symbol of new beginnings and of purity. It suggests endless possibilities and a unique innocence. The early morning is a time of peace and quiet. It is a perfect time for reflection and is symbolic of the birth of man in Eden. Thus, some consider the morning to be a time of blessings and of promise. If the setting of your dream is the morning, then its interpretation should be made in the light of positive aspirations and optimism.

Moth

A moth is not very attractive, desirable, or known for many positive attributes. There is the story of a moth being attracted to the flame, which got too close to the flame and was destroyed. The moth in your dream may be pointing out a personal weakness or may be bringing to light a deception in your life. It could be suggesting that you are being led to a place where you will be hurt unless you recognize the danger. Since dreams are very rarely literal, the danger could be emotional or psychological, rather than physical.

Mother

The relationship that we have with our mother is the most psychologically significant relationship of all. Rarely all good or all bad, our mothers always invoke powerful emotions. We may dream about our mothers in many different forms. She may be disguised in our dreams, and it is our job to find her in there. If you are dreaming about your mother, you may be addressing some issues or concerns in your dream, or your dream may be based on a valuable memory. The general image of "mother" in a dream may symbolize a variety of feelings and ideas: caring, nurturing, love, acceptance, hard work, sacrifice, martyrdom, etc. The mother in your dream could also represent "collective unconscious," the source of the "water of life," and the yin. Carl Jung suggests that women in dreams represent our collective unconscious and men the collective consciousness. Thus, the woman is that force, or current, inside of you that nudges you on and inspires you. It is your intuition and the knowledge that in not necessarily attached to words. Men, on the other hand, represent the active part of us that uses the information received to create the physical reality of our lives. When the two are working together well, we have balance and experience awareness leading to peace and productivity. *See also:* Parents

Mountain

Climbing a real mountain is not always fun but it usually challenging and rewarding. Some say that the mountain may represent spirituality while others suggest mental development and self-awareness. The most literal interpretation of climbing a mountain is that it represents attainment of goals. If you are ascending a mountain you may be working hard and trying to accomplish your goals, whether they are spiritual, emotional, or material.

Music

Hearing music in your dreams has positive connotations. Music is healing to the soul, and as you are listening to it in your dream, you may be connected to the wonderful, creative spirit or flow of life suggesting a degree of inner harmony and emotional expression. *See also:* Melody/Song

Nails

Hammering of nails in a dream might represent feelings of anger and hostility, or it might symbolize hard work and honorable endeavors. Additionally, nails may have some sexual connotations. A man may be expressing some repressed anxiety about sexual potency while a woman may be expressing her unconscious abhorrence of sex.

Night

A nighttime setting is common to many dreams. However, extreme darkness suggests that you are hiding something or are unwilling to see things clearly. You may be the type who likes to ignore, minimize, or hide problems. The darkness represents a lack of awareness and illumination. If you honestly look at the content of your dream, you may be able to identify some areas of your life or personal experience that need warmth, light, and airing.

Nightmare

If you have nightmares, try to understand the fears and the events in those dreams. They suggest that you may be holding on to traumatic or guilt-based conflicts. You may have a lot of powerful negative feelings that require reconciliation. If nightmares continue for an extended period of time, the individual should consider obtaining professional counseling services. Nightmares are a direct result of overwhelming feelings of fear and helplessness, or a result of an unprocessed traumatic experience. A nightmare is any dream that wakes you up because of its frightening and overwhelming images.

Nudity

Being naked in a dream suggests vulnerability and exposure. It could be compensation for what is going on in daily life. Are you very guarded and unwilling to let people see the "real" you, or are you feeling embarrassment as a result of a mistake or emotional reaction? With this dream, the unconscious might be encouraging you to become more open with your feelings and more accessible emotionally. Additionally, if you see yourself naked in inappropriate places, your rebellious side may be coming through and with it some fear that people may not accept you for what you really are. Nudity in sexual dreams has its own meaning. For suggestions, please see Sex.

Numbers

Interpreting numbers that we see in dreams may be difficult. Their meaning may be very personal, such as a reflection of financial concern or any other area of daily life represented by numbers. One way to interpret numbers is to try to see how they are specifically related to you. For example, if you see number 25 in your dream and it does not make any sense to you at first, think about the meaningful numbers in your life that add up to 25. Maybe your house number is 12 and your parent's house number is 13. Together they make 25, and this dream could have been addressing issues about your relationship with your parents.

On the other hand, numbers in dreams may represent global concepts and point to collective dilemmas. Even numbers may represent the feminine and odd numbers the masculine. Some interesting interpretations of common numbers include the following:

Number two—psychic development and doubling; something new coming up with the potential for building.

Number three—the trinity; it is an active or a process number (something is going on in the psyche).

Number four—completion and femininity.

Number five—life force; refers to the five fingers and five appendages of the body.

Number seven—sacred number in Christianity and Judaism; the highest stage of illumination and spirituality.

Number twelve—represents time and may mark the most important cycles in life.

Obesity

As usual, the interpretation of this dream depends on you. You may be concerned about your looks and fear that you are becoming fat. Be realistic in regard to this area of your life. If you are very thin and cannot stop worrying about your weight, you should see a doctor. Psychologically speaking, obesity usually is a sign that the individual has issues with self-esteem and personal power. In dreams about obesity, fat emotionally insulates us from others and isolates us physically.

Ocean

It traditionally represents our great unconscious, memories, emotions, and individual soul and collective experiences. Look at all of the details in this dream. Is the water clear or murky? Is it calm or turbulent? Are you catching fish, or are you stranded and afraid? Look, listen, and try to comprehend the messages in this dream. No one is in a better position to give meaning to your dreams than you. Concentrate and learn for yourself. *See also:* Water

Octopus

You may say, "Who dreams of an octopus?" but people do, and you probably did if you are looking up this dream symbol. Frightening dreams involving an octopus may point to unhealthy attachments and entanglements in daily life. If the dream content was not frightening or disturbing, it may reflect your involvement in many different activities or adventures. *See also:* Animals

Oil
The content of the dream will tell you if its message is about wealth, religion, spirituality, or sex. Traditionally, oil is used as a part of many religious sacraments. It represents wealth for people who own it, and it also may have sexual connotations. What does it mean for you?

Old Man/Old Woman
Carl Jung said that the wise old man is the "archetype of the spirit" and the "speaking fountainhead of the soul." Dreaming about him may be an attempt to bring oneself into awareness of the larger meaning of one's life. Old people in dreams represent wisdom and maturity. They may appear in our dreams at times of confusion, when we lack direction, or when we need consultation and help in decision-making. *See also:* Aging

Orange (color)
The color orange corresponds to the second chakra and, at times, may be associated with our reproductive system. The second chakra is said to be responsible for our reproductive health and has something to do with our sexual expression. Consider your sexual and reproductive health and then make other and more personal associations in order to obtain a good interpretation of the color orange.

Oven

The most obvious symbolism is that of a womb. You may be having some fears or anticipation in regard to having children. A warm oven is said to have "fruitful," or positive, connotations, while a cold oven the opposite. Of course, an oven may simply represent housekeeping and cooking. *See also:* Kitchen

Owl

It is another symbol for the unconscious. It usually represents wisdom and virtue, and your unconscious may be giving you important messages, so pay attention to the details in the dream. In the American Indian tradition, the owl is considered to be the eagle of the night. Dreaming about owls is a powerful dream that may indicate that changes are on the way. Superstition-based dream interpretations suggest that dreaming about an owl is a negative omen, which indicates a reversal in good fortune. An owl in the house predicts family arguments and chasing it away might cause things to work out for the best.

Oyster

An oyster in your dream may have sexual connotations. It usually represents the female sex organ or, if eaten by a man, may represent his ability or desire to perform well sexually. Oysters are also considered symbols of humility and wisdom. Their meaning is associated with that of pearls. The most negative interpretation is that the oyster represents a well-guarded individual; a person who has shut himself off from others. Attempt to connect some of these ideas to your emotional life and overall experiences and keep in mind the setting, context, and outcome of the dream.

Packing

This dream, like all dreams, could have several different meanings. If you are packing your stuff and storing it or packing to move, you may be concerned about significant changes that are going on in your life. Otherwise, your unconscious may be organizing and letting go of emotional "baggage." Some other interpretations say that dreaming about packing is simply a hint from your unconscious that you are involved in too many activities and may need to pack some of them up and put them away.

Pain

When considering the interpretation of feeling pain in your dream, first look at you physical health. If you are feeling pain in your daily life, it may carry over into your dream state. Additionally, if the pain is emotional in nature, question the painful feelings and attempt to identify their source. The dream state is usually a safe way to experience negative feelings with which you may not want to deal.

Panic

The feeling of panic suggests lack of control and confusion. If the primary emotion in your dream is panic, consider the details and try to understand its cause. Do you feel fear, a sense of confused helplessness, or were you unable to make a quick and accurate decision? Answering these questions will enable you to understand the message in this dream.

Pants

Clothing generally represents the roles that we play in life and how others perceive us. If putting on pants or changing your pants, plays a major part in your dream you may be questioning your role at work, home, or in any other area of life. The physical look of the pants, who is wearing them, and the emotional content of the dream will give you clues to its meaning. If you were trying to cover up your genitalia, then the dream may be bringing up sexual issues.

Paralysis

Dreaming that you or someone else is paralyzed could be very frightening. Depending on the details of your dream and your current situation in life, there are several different, but equally reasonable interpretations. The fear that paralyzes you in the dream may be symbolic of the fear that you are experiencing in daily life. You may feel somewhat unable to change a current situation, which may manifest itself in your dream as a form of paralysis. In addition, this dream may be cautioning you to stay still and do nothing for now in regard to a real-life situation that is on your mind and may be problematic for you. In the dream you may be "frozen with fear" and it is up to you decipher what that fear is and what it represents.

Parents

In this dream you may be expressing feelings and concerns about your parents that you could not express in daily life. Some believe that this dream usually has nothing to do with your parents, but rather the male and female sides of personality or self. The father may represent the expressive, creative, and protective sides of God, while the mother His receptive and nurturing side. Carl Jung suggests that women in dreams represent our collective unconscious and men our collective consciousness. Thus, the woman is that force, or current, inside of you that urges you on and inspires you. This knowledge is intuitive and unexpressed by words. Men, on the other hand, represent the active part of us that uses the information received to create the physical reality of our lives. When the two are working together well we have balance and experience awareness leading to peace and productivity. *See also:* Mother, Father

Parking Lot/Garage

These are interesting symbols and many people have requested including the dictionary. Traveling is a very common theme in our dreams, and traveling in a car the most common. Traveling in a vehicle generally represents our journey through life, or a portion of it. Finding yourself in a garage or a parking lot can be interpreted in several different ways. First, consider the content of your dream and your current dilemma or situation in life. The parked car could represent a period of inactivity and indecision in your life. The dream could be pointing out that you have been idle for a period of time and that it may be a good time to "get a move on." The more positive interpretation of this dream may be that the parked car is symbolic of a reflective period or mood. You may be in "park" for a while so that you can rest, relax, regroup, and think things over.

Peacock

We have all heard the expression "as proud as a peacock." Dreaming about this bird may be a symbolic conveying of beauty and pride. We all know that some pride may be a good thing, but too much pride is not so good. Consider all of the details of your dream and try to understand the message. Is the peacock in your dream beautiful and proud, yet unassuming, or is he noisily flaunting his beauty to all that are willing to look?

Pen/Pencil

Having a pen or a pencil in your dream may be symbolic of your need to communicate with yourself or others. Our ability to communicate through written language is a vitally important and necessary part of life. When we take our pen and write a check to pay bills, it can still be considered a form of communication! Writing is a form of self-expression, providing us with a way to think and express our thoughts. Dreams with writing tools in them may be an encouragement for you to write and communicate. Whether you need to communicate with yourself or others, in private or professional life, is up to you to determine.

Penguin

The penguin is an interesting earth-bound bird that lives in and around the ocean. As a dream symbol it may represent concrete thinking, feelings of being burdened by unwanted emotions, lethargy, and a need to achieve balance. Think about your dream and see if any of these ideas are relevant to you. Superstition-based dream interpretation books say that the penguin indicates that your problems are not as serious as you may think them to be.

Penis

The male sex organ is symbolic of fertility, power, and energy. Your gender and sexual orientation play a part when interpreting this dream. Are you dealing with issues of sexual orientation, power, or aggression? Answering these questions will enable you to interpret your dream. *See also:* Sex

People

Usually our dreams are filled with people. We dream about our families, our friends, our neighbors, and our classmates. We dream about strangers, colleges, famous people, teachers, and, at times, our supposed enemies. Each dream is very special and carries its own unique message. When interpreting a dream with people in it, consider all of the details and the feelings in the dream. If the person is known to you, think about your relationship with him or her and the issues that the dream has brought up. We learn about ourselves through others, and probably our most valuable possessions are our relationships. Some believe that the strangers in your dreams represent different parts of yourself and are extensions and projections of your own personality. Many people believe that their dreams can predict the future. When they have negative or frightening dreams, they become anxious about the future. Alternatively, when their dreams are a form of wish-fulfillment, the dreamers become very excited and are hopeful that the dream will come true. Most dreams are not prophetic but are psychological or spiritual in nature. Their primary function may be to help us live better in the present, rather than the future. *See also:* Ex-Boyfriend/Girlfriend, Siblings, Child, Parent, Mother, Father

Phoenix

In Greek mythology, the Phoenix was a bird with great beauty, splendor, and longevity. The legend tells us that the Phoenix lived for five hundred years and then retreated to make a nest where she would die. She made a nest of aromatic twigs that would burn from the heat of its own body. The Phoenix is said to rise from its own ashes. It comes alive though the transforming power of fire and it lives again in full splendor. In the Middle Ages, the Phoenix was often used as a symbol for Christ, as He was resurrected. This legendary bird is an archetypal dream symbol that brings us positive and powerful images of rebirth. If you dream of the Phoenix, it is most likely that you are receiving messages from the unconscious that are telling you that new life and new beginnings are always possible. This bird is a reminder that we have internal powers of regeneration and that we have the power to change things for the better. As you are interpreting this dream, try to visualize a great bird rising up from fire and ash. It is a powerful image, whether produced by a dream or visualization.

Photograph/Picture

Seeing old or even unfamiliar pictures in your dream may be a reflection of how you remember certain parts of your life. These pictures may represent longing for a time that has passed. However, other interpretations can be made. Although this dream may be difficult to interpret, the dreamer may need to put significant amount of effort into its understanding. Some believe that since a photograph represents something real, it could represent a deception or distortion of some kind. Someone may be trying to sell something to you and is covering up the truth, or you may be doing the covering yourself. New Age thinking points out that dreaming of pictures means you have not learned a particular lesson in life. The dream may be calling attention to past events and reminding you that you are making the same errors all over again.

Piano

The piano symbolizes music, harmony, and expression. All types of sounds may be uplifting symbols of spiritual awareness. Superstition-based dream interpretation books say that the piano is an omen for a good financial period in your life, and moving a piano represents solid achievements on the part of the dreamer. *See also:* Music, Melody/Song

Pier

Sometimes a dreamer may stand on a pier looking out over the ocean (or other large body of water), sometimes waiting for a ship or a boat. The water symbolizes the unconscious and our emotions. It could also be considered the "water of life," with meaning ranging form the simplest (as the necessity for life) to the most profound (life itself and all of its complexities). Its meaning can be drawn though analysis of your current situation and internal dynamics. If we are waiting for the opportunity to begin a new adventure, it could be reflected in this dream. Additionally, you may have a desire to get to know yourself better, to explore your own unconscious, and to grow in an emotional, psychological, or spiritual way. You are standing on a pier because you need or want to go on a journey in daily real life or an internal journey to your own unconscious.

Pig

Dreaming about this animal in your dream forces you to consider the negative characteristics of yourself or others. There are not many positive characteristics associated with pigs. In some cultures pigs are considered to be very "dirty" and unfit for human consumption. At times, men are referred to as "pigs" for their sexual desires or attitudes. Pigs are also associated with other negative characteristics: greed, stubbornness, and gluttony. Are you (or someone important to you) being "hoggish" with money, time, food, energy, or personal possessions? Superstition-based dream interpretations say that the pig in a dream may suggest a frustrating time in family affairs but success in business. In some cultures the pig is a symbol of prosperity because the families owning one are assured of food for an entire year. As a dream symbol it represents "korist," which is loosely translated to mean a valuable possession or event. *Also see:* Animals

Pink

Pink usually symbolizes health and good feelings. It is a traditionally a feminine color, and some feel that it connotes love. Pink is soft and fuzzy, like girls!

Planets

Dreaming about planets could represent desire to explore either our internal world or the world of our egos (the external or physical world). Planets could also represent deeper things such as the way that we relate to ourselves. They can say something about the relationship that exists between our soul and ego. An orbiting planet could represent your ego. It is traveling around the sun (i.e., soul) and the entire thing could be a huge circle that is You. If this sounds like a very far out idea, well, it may be! However, if what Carl Jung said is true, all dream images bring us back to issues of self-identity and a more evolved and profound understanding of self.

Pluto (Hades)

Pluto, or Hades, is synonymous with hell. Pluto is the brother of Zeus and Poseidon and the ruler of the underworld, or the land of the dead. The kingdom of the dead is located underneath the surface of the earth. It is not only the holding place for the eternally damned, but is symbolic of metamorphoses, mineral wealth, germination, and the transition from death to life. From a psychoanalytic point of view, Pluto may represent the deepest and the oldest part of the psyche. It may be the holding place of the darkest and most negative and disturbing elements of the individual. The most destructive emotions and the greatest fears may be hidden there. However, this dark part of the psyche may also hold the greatest amount of transformative energy and power. As the unconscious demons begin to surface and are processed and then assimilated by the conscious mind, the individual begins to develop and experience feelings of completeness and wholeness. Astrologically, Pluto is symbolic of radical reconstruction that rejects harmful elements and is built on a solid foundation. Seeing Pluto in dreams seems to be an extremely valuable message from the unconscious. It suggests that the dreamer needs to contemplate and to explore his inner world, to face his fears and negative traits, to travel inward, and then to emerge stronger and more alive than he was before the psychic or soulful journey began.

Pockets

From a Freudian point of view, pockets may symbolize the female reproductive organs. However, for many people this dream may have an entirely different meaning. The pockets in your dreams could represent those things that you keep just for yourself: your memory, your secrecy, your valuable possessions, or your inner resources. If you were hiding your hands in the pockets, it suggests that you may feel a degree of helplessness or guilt in regard to some situation in daily life.

Police

Dreaming about the police could symbolize many different things, so please consider all of the details carefully. If the police are chasing you, it suggests that you may be feeling some guilt about something that you have done or have been thinking of doing. The police could be addressing karmic law as well as the laws in our physical world. If you are feeling that you can't meet all of your obligations and fear repercussions due to an unmet commitment, the police may be an unwelcome sight. On a more positive note and depending on the details of your dream, the police could symbolize support and protection. Your emotional response to the dream will provide you with good clues to interpreting this dream accurately. Old dream interpretation books say that dreaming about police is an indication that you will obtain unexpected assistance with a current problem.

Pool

For many people, swimming pools are associated with summer fun, vacations, rest, and relaxation. Interpret your dream based on its content and see if any these positive feelings are being conveyed to you. All bodies of water represent our emotions and unconscious. The manner in which they are presented depends on the dreamer and on the details of the dream. *See also:* Water, Ocean, River

Porcupine

Old dream interpretation books say the porcupine in your dreams is an omen of good news and bad news. Good things may happen to you, but they will carry difficulties with them. From a more pragmatic point of view, porcupines are cute but untouchable animals. As a dream symbol it may represent a situation or a person in your life who fits that description.

Poverty

Most spiritual paths respect or require material poverty so that spiritual wealth may be acquired. "Blessed are the poor," said Matthew in 5:3. In medieval times they called it a "perfect poverty," where the individual would give up material wealth and seek spiritual development. In Islam, this quest for spiritual development through material poverty is called "faqr." If in real life you are not poor, dreaming that you live in poverty or experiencing great poverty in your dreams may be considered a dream of the contrary or a compensatory dream. Superstition-based dream interpretations would say that if you are poor in your dream you will gain material luck in the near future. Dreaming about poverty may be interpreted in light of what is going on in your daily life (as may most dream interpretations). Thus, if you are on an upward swing and are doing really well financially, you may have a compensatory dream of being poor. This is simply a way by which you obtain psychic balance. However, if you are experiencing financial stress, dreaming of being poor may be a way for you to cope with fear and anxiety that you are unable to cope with directly.

Pregnancy

If you are afraid of being pregnant, you may dream of it often. At times, women learn about their pregnancy in their dreams. Your mind knows about everything that is going on in your body even if you are not consciously aware of it. However, don't panic! You could also be pregnant with ideas! Old dream interpretation books say that a dream about pregnancy is a good omen for women, and an improvement in her intimate relationship is forthcoming. For a man, it is a warning against casual sex.

Priest

The priest in your dream could represent spiritual needs, your conscience, a desire to be virtuous, inner guidance, or your higher self. This dream could be comforting if it reassures you that there is safety and strength in spiritual forces. Please remember that dream interpretation is very, very personal. Some people may have had negative experiences with clergy, and in that case the dream may have an entirely different tone. The spiritual forces represented in this dream could be intrinsic, revealing your own spiritual qualities, strengths, and abilities, or they could represent the spiritual forces around you.

Puppy

Puppies may represent playfulness, dependency, and carefree fun. Please look up *Dog* in order to obtain a full range of possible interpretations.

Purple

Purple is usually the color of royalty, high rank, or dignity. It is a strong color that can not be ignored. Likewise, most people have a strong opinion of purple: they really like it or vehemently dislike it. To some people, purple has spiritual connotations. The Catholic Church uses it at funerals and around Easter time. It represents spiritual and personal transformation. Purple could also represent higher consciousness and spiritual protection. A version of purple is also the color of the crown Chakra. When interpreting this color consider all of the details in the dream and try to make connections between the above mentioned ideas and your current issues. *See also:* Colors

Pyramid

This ancient and powerful symbol has general meaning for all and specific meaning for the dreamer. It represents the coming together of the world of man with that of God; the material with the spiritual. The purpose of the pyramids was to bury the dead and to assist them into reaching eternity. In this way, the pyramids were holy places and their architecture and mysticism continues to amaze and to intrigue us. In order to understand its symbolism; consider your current accomplishments and breakthroughs. If you accomplished a personal goal and feel a sense of wholeness, this dream symbol may be an affirmation of those feelings. The pyramid could also represent larger goals and deepest strivings. Whether they represent fulfilled or incomplete goals, a pyramid seems to be a very positive dream symbol.

Quarrel

If you are quarreling or arguing in your dream you may be experiencing some inner conflict. The quarrel may reflect your own inability to resolve important issues, ideas, or values. Most likely, you may be experiencing ongoing difficulty with making decisions, cannot accept authority, or you may have carried an argument from your daily life into your dream. Very old dream interpretation books say that quarreling is a *dream of the contrary* and that you will have peace and harmony with your loved ones.

Queen

In African folklore, the King is said to be "the one who holds all life, human and cosmic, in his hands; the keystone of society and the universe." In the modern world, we may not associate the King with ultimate power, knowledge, or wisdom. However, historically the mythical King was highly spiritual, was the center of the wheel of life, and was said to have a regulatory function in the cosmos. Psychologically, the king and the queen are said to be the "archetypes of human perfection." As a dream symbol, you can understand the king or queen in your dream by realizing that they represent your ability for independence, self-understanding, and self-determination. They also represent inner wealth that will enable you to be your best and help you to achieve your goals. Consciously, you may never have the desire to be a king or queen, but psychologically, these figures are symbolic of our highest potential and our desire to be the "king or queen" of our own world and our own lives. On rare occasions and depending on the details of the dream, the king and queen may represent a powerful force that is unkind and tyrannical.

Quicksand

You may be experiencing feelings of helplessness and an inability to get out of a situation in your daily life. This common sense approach can easily be applied and with some effort you can examine your feelings and actions symbolized in this dream.

Quilt

It is usually something warm and pretty that we cover ourselves with for comfort. The different parts of a quilt may represent the harmonious coexistence of many aspects of your life. Your unconscious may be comforting you in this dream by saying, "You are doing a good job. Keep going!" If you lack comfort and harmony then this dream may be compensatory and providing you with that which you need more of in daily life.

Rabbit

Rabbits are cuddly and cute. They are known for their quickness but not their keen perceptions or intelligence. In our dreams, rabbits can represent luck, quickness, fertility, pregnancy, or magic. However, they can also symbolize the dreamer's lack of consciousness or awareness. Rabbits as dream symbols might suggest to the dreamer that sometimes he reacts too quickly to life's situations and that more thought and planning may be needed.

Race

Are you competing or running from or to something? In order to have a good understanding of this dream you should consider those factors. If you are simply running, it may be an indication that you need to slow down in your everyday life. If you are competing, you need to consider your competitive drive and realistically look at the current challenges. If you are running in a race and win, your unconscious may be expressing confidence that you may or may not feel in the wakened state. Running in your dreams may also symbolize the energy levels, the strength, or the force that you have to get through life.

Rain

Interpretation is contingent on your current circumstances as well as the kind of rain that is falling. Rain naturally cleans, refreshes, and "provides life-giving moisture." Depending on the dreamer, it could suggest a period of renewal and fertility (reproduction or creativity). However, dark clouds and a heavy downpour indicate feelings of isolation and helplessness. On the other hand, the heavy downpour could represent unconscious materials and emotions attempting to enter the dreamer's conscious mind. *See also:* Water

Rainbow

Rainbows are colorful bridges that fall across the sky, but we cannot walk across them (or use them to get to our pot of gold). Currently you may experience great joy and have extraordinary or even magical ideas, but remember that you cannot walk across the rainbow bridge, so stay well-grounded. Usually a rainbow follows a rainstorm. If so, you have weathered a difficult time that is coming to an end; this dream symbol may represent your optimism. Generally, rainbows make people smile and feel happy. Thus, some may consider this dream a sign of your good luck.

Rape

Dreaming about being raped is a nightmare that inflicts fear and anxiety upon recall. Since rape is a brutal and deeply personal violation, it suggests that the dreamer may be feeling robbed of options and negated as a human being. In a dream, as in real life, rape has very little to do with sex. It is about power, control, anger, and other very destructive emotions. In order to understand this dream, you may need to think about the areas of your life that causes you great anxiety and fear. If you are superstitious, take this dream as a warning. Take precautions, protect yourself emotionally and physically, and don't engage in careless behaviors. If you were a rape victim, the traumatic nature of this experience may cause you to have a dream like this from time to time.

Rats

They are unpleasant and symbolize danger, poverty, filth, and illness. Your unconscious mind may be bringing up unpleasant images due to a disturbance in daily life. The dream's purpose is to make you aware of negative feelings that may encourage you to directly deal with the negativity in your life. Dreaming about rats leaves the dreamer feeling apprehensive and disgusted. Attempt to connect these feelings with those things that produce this type of anxiety during the day.

Relationships

It is common to dream about our relationships. You can interpret this dream by remembering the details and comparing them to the realities of your daily life. In your dream state you may be experiencing some wish-fulfillment or confronting things that you would normally ignore. Some say that relationships with strangers in your dream state represent the different sides of your personality. *See also:* Ex-boyfriend/girlfriend

Resurrection

The word resurrection has positive and miracles implications. Jesus was resurrected on the third day, and He also resurrected Lazarus. The theme of resurrection is explored in all cultures and religions. It is always something awesome and wondrous. Dreaming about resurrection may point to the awakening of your spiritual nature. If you came into knowledge or "enlightenment" that you never had before, the dream could be referring to the resurrection of the spirit. This dream could also represent insight or a new energy. Some think that dreams about resurrection are symbolic of reincarnation.

Right

The right side of the brain is associated with fluid intelligence, nonverbal reasoning, and creativity. In your dream you may be concerned with direction or being right. Either way right usually has positive connotations. You may be sending messages to yourself that you are on a right path or doing the right thing.

Ring

Are you dreaming about ornamental jewelry or merely noise? If you are dreaming the former, the ring may be symbolic of your commitments and promises. The ring can been seen from a larger point of view as a circle, which is a symbol of completion and wholeness. If the ring is a noise, it can be interpreted as an attention-seeking message. Consider those things that you have been ignoring or unwilling to look at and examine the details of your dream. Some people believe that a type of pleasant ringing may be a "joyful" noise and that it is the sound of God. In that case this dream is a real blessing!

River

Water sustains life and is the most abundant compound in all living things. It may represent the flow of your energies, the path of your life, or the passage of time. It also may be symbolic of your emotional well-being. Examine the details of your dream. Is the water clear or murky? Is it fast-moving, turbulent, or stagnant? Are you just floating along its currents or actively controlling your movements? Consider these factors and see how they can be associated with daily life. *See also:* Water, Ocean

Road

It usually symbolizes the journey that we take to achieve our goals. The road in the dream represents a road in your life. It could be the road to your heart, spirit, or mind. Consider the kind of road that you were on and try to see how it relates to your daily realities. If the road is straight, well-marked, and lit, it may an affirmation that you are moving in the right directions. If there are many obstacles and the road is very hard, consider your options. *See also:* Car, Travel

Rocks

The connotation of this symbol as with all other dream symbols, depends on the details and the mood of the dream. The rock or rocks in your dream could represent a variety of different ideas, but it usually has something to do with matters of this physical world. Rocks generally do not represent emotional, psychological, or spiritual issues. Rather, they may represent earthiness, sturdiness, stability, and a solid foundation. On the other hand, they could represent physical obstacles or difficulties which the dreamer may need to overcome.

Roller Coaster

Dreaming about a roller coaster ride seems to symbolize the emotional ups and downs that a person is experiencing. Although this ride can be fun, it can also seem out-of-control and even be a frightening experience. As a dream symbols it suggests that the dreamer may need to achieve greater emotional balance. The sever changes in mood and temperament are draining and unproductive and may be highlighted by the roller coaster dream. If the dream is feeling emotionally flat and apathetic, then this dreamer may be a form of compensation.

Roof

At times, a roof represents the crown choker. It may represent a barrier between states of consciousness or be symbolic of your ideology and philosophy. If you are dreaming about a leaky roof, new information may be trying to get into your conscious awareness. On a more pragmatic note, the roof in your dreams could be bringing up issues of protection and materialistic comfort (a roof over your head). *See also:* House

Rooster

The meaning of this symbol could be very much like that of chickens. However, the rooster represents male energy and possibly aggression. If you ever observed a rooster in a hen house, you would notice that they are very aggressive, demanding, and territorial. This dream may be pointing to these characteristics inside of you or others. A rooster crowing is a traditional wake-up call on a farm while in literature it is sometimes symbolic of some type of a warning. If the rooster in your dream is crowing, think about your current situation and if this dream is a wake-up call in regard to a situation in your life. *See also:* Chickens

Rosary

In the Western world, the rosary is generally though of as a Catholic prayer item. Catholics say the rosary by repetitive prayer and meditation, with the focus on the Blessed Mother or the Virgin Mary. However, most religions have their own prayer beads or rosary. A rosary consists of pearls or beads linked together by a thread. The Hindu rosary has 50 beads, the Buddhist rosary 108 beads, and the Muslim rosary 99 beads. In Africa, some groups have a rosary made out of human teeth. Prayers and specific meditations of each religion are different and there are theological reasons for the number of beads. Rosaries may come in different colors, sizes, and designs. However, the central purpose, which is to pray repetitively and to meditate, is the same across all religions that use them as a prayer tool. If you are seeing rosary beads in your dream it suggests that prayer and meditation is needed in your daily life. The unconscious generally provides us with helpful images that are not always difficult to understand. Thus, if you are not a prayerful person, the rosary in your dreams may be encouraging you to begin a more introspective and meditative life. Think about the rosary in your dream and try to decipher what it means to you and how you may incorporate meditation and peaceful reflection into your conscious life.

Rose

Most flowers are seen as friendly dream symbols. Roses may have their own special meaning and could represent femininity, beauty, love, or romance. Roses may have some spiritual significance as well. They are used when expressing both positive and negative emotions. They unfold and can be considered symbols of innocence. The color of the rose, as well as the details of the dream, should be considered when making an interpretation. (i.e., white—purity; red—passion; pink—romance and love; black—death.) *See also:* Flower

Running

Dreaming of running competitively should be distinguished from dreams which have you running to or from something. If you are simply running with no goal, it may be an indication that you need to slow down in your every day life. If you are competing, you need to consider your recent rivalries and realistically look at the current challenges. If you are running in a race and win, your unconscious may be expressing confidence that you may or may not feel in the wakened state. Running in your dreams may also symbolize the energy levels, the strength, or the force that you have to get through life. *See also:* Race

Sacrifice

Before we can nourish others, we first need to nourish ourselves. Making sacrifices is human, but when we do too much for the world and not enough for ourselves, we are left feeling neglected and weak. Martyrdom is not fun and martyrs are at times annoying. This dream may be suggesting to you that you need to prioritize. Eliminate things in your life that are not necessary and continuously drag you down. Also, consider the fact that whatever is constantly requiring you to make personal sacrifices may not be in your best interest or conducive to your health or happiness. Superstition-based dream interpretations say that dreaming about sacrifice is a *dream of the contrary* and that you will be enriched in the near future.

Saint

Dreaming about saints usually has spiritual implications. You may have traveled to another plain and are having a wonderful, very meaningful spiritual experience. For those who cannot accept this possibility, the unconscious may be relaying some feelings of pressure or possibly the need to sacrifice on some level in daily life. *See also:* Priest, God

Salt

Salt is one of the most abundant chemicals on Earth. Dreaming about it suggests that you may be thinking about or desiring those things that are dependable and, at the same time, exciting (salt = spice of life). If you associate an individual with the salt in your dreams you may be giving that person the attributes that were just mentioned.

Satan

Seeing or interacting with the devil in your dreams may have several different meanings and the interpretation depends on the details of the dream. However, it almost always points to something negative and disturbing in your personality, daily life, or environment. Carl Jung called such dark figures "the shadow" and said that they represent the negative ego personality and qualities which are painful and regrettable. You may have dark thoughts or have engaged in negative actions and now are experiencing guilt, fear, and anxiety. Dream interpretations based on folklore say that seeing the Satan in your dreams may be a warning about poor health, and if the dream persists, you should get a physical checkup. *See also:* Devil

Saturn (Cronos)

Saturn is a Roman deity representing the Golden Age. He is associated with the Greek god Cronos. Cronos was a Titan, the son of Uranus and the father of Zeus (Jupiter). Cronos dethroned his father and was later dethroned by Zeus. Thus, from a psychoanalytic point of view, dreaming about Saturn may be symbolic of some aspects of the Oedipus complex. It may bring up the desire to challenge authority and gain personal power and identity. Astrologically, Saturn represents a wide range of positive and negative attributes. He represents barriers, misfortune, fixation and impotence, as well as loyalty, righteousness, consistency, knowledge and self-denial.

Saturn symbolizes man's ability to recognize the difficulties of life and to confront the impulsive and passion motivated lifestyle. Dreaming about Saturn, may be an unconscious message regarding self-restrain and a need for a more intellectual, moral and spiritual life. Also, Saturn's influence has a way of amplifying reality. If there is melancholy or despair, it remains fixed. Thus, dreaming of Saturn might call your attention to unpleasant aspects of life or to self-negating emotions. However, the psyche may be providing you with knowledge that can be used to motivate and transform current reality through hard work and self-discipline.

School

This dream may be interpreted on several different levels. If you are the student, you may be feeling inadequate or lack self confidence. Either way, going to school or attending class in a dream is your unconscious reminder that there is a need for new learning and that you may have not learned an important lesson. School may not always be a positive experience, but it is always necessary. Ask yourself what do you need to learn more about? If you were a teacher in your dream, you may be dealing with issues of authority. From a spiritual point of view, some believe that in the dream state an individual may travel to an inner plane or the spiritual realm, where they can attend classes which assist in spiritual growth and development.

Scorpion

Dreaming about a scorpion may be symbolic of something in your environment which is hurtful, dangerous, and "stinging." It may represent bitter words and very negative attitudes. Superstition-based dream interpretation books say that a scorpion may constitute a warning. It further states that if the scorpion in your dream bit you, you will overcome your problems. However, if you killed the scorpion, be exceptionally careful around people who are not your friends, or are false friends. Some believe that the scorpion is a symbol of transformation.

Sea
Waters generally symbolize the emotions and the unconscious. They could also represent the collective unconscious or your soul experiences. All dream interpretations depend on the individuals personal belief system and life experiences. *See also:* Water, Ocean

Seed
Seeds symbolize new opportunities and new beginnings. Just as a seed is the beginning of a new life (or its earliest stage), your unconscious may be telling you that the ideas you have planted are beginning to germinate. Additionally, past experiences and hard work may be leading to new opportunities or possibilities.

Sex
It is very difficult to name just a few possible interpretations for this dream. It is so complex that interpretations vary with each dreamer and situation in the dream. A sexual dream may be about physical pleasure, but it may also be about power, control, manipulation, virility, and effectiveness. It may be a form of wish fulfillment or a memory, or compensation for a lack in daily life. In most cases, it is not a predic-

tion of things to come in the near future. For some more clues, also see Intercourse and People.

Sharks

Please remember that the water in your dreams may be a statement about your emotions and the unconscious. Sharks, water-dwelling animals, could represent unpleasant emotions or difficult and painful materials coming up from the unconscious. You may feel some emotional upset, and the shark could be the symbol of the perceived emotional danger. Old dream interpretation books say that sharks may represent dishonest friends or reflect financial troubles. *See also:* Animals

Ship

As mentioned in all relevant dream symbols, bodies of water represent your unconscious, your emotions, and your accumulated soul experiences. The ship in your dream could represent you and the ways in which you navigate thought these parts of yourself. When interpreting this dream, consider the kind of voyage and the type of ship. Some dream interpretation books say that if the voyage is calm you should go forward with your plans. However, if it is a very stormy voyage, get ready for an emotional upset (or challenge). *See also:* Boat

Shirt

Any type of clothing, especially shirts, generally represent our worldly appearance or status. At times, they may represent our attitudes toward ourselves and others. Mostly, they represent the way that we appear to the world. They are not symbolic of our private self but rather of our public self. A poor man wears a different shirt than a rich man. A doctor wears a different shirt than a carpenter. The type of clothing that we wear varies form situation to situation. The type of shirts being worn will give you clues to the meaning of the dream and to your unconscious ideas about yourself and others. If you are putting on many shirts, it suggests that you are somewhat confused about what you want to be or how you want others to see you. *See also:* Clothing

Shoe

First consider if you are currently having problems with your feet that are being carried over into the dream state. Otherwise, we only wear shoes that fit us well. Thus, you may be expressing unconscious feelings of self assurance or confidence. You may have issues concerning your self-identify, but if the details of this dream are supporting, you may be reassuring yourself that you are on the right path and have mastered a degree of self awareness.

Shooting

Shooting someone or being shot yourself is a fearful and violent dream experience. It may reflect aggression, powerlessness, release of strong and dangerous emotions, and/or symbolize a conclusive event in a particular situation or relationship. *See also:* Guns

Shopping

For most of us shopping is not simply a necessity but a favorite pastime. It is a source of pain, pleasure, recreation, and, at times, "quality time" with family or friends. Depending on the details in the dream and its emotional background, dreaming about going shopping may have several different connotations. Generally, if shopping in your dream is not a source of great stress and confusion, it suggests that those things which you need are available to you. Your environment may have readily available emotional, psychological, spiritual, or physical support. However, you may need to learn exactly where to look, how to select what you need, and when to make a wise investment. This dream calls upon you to know yourself. Before you can ask for or get what you need, you first need to accurately identify it.

Sibling

It is very common for us to dream about all different types of people. Siblings are a fantastic source of dream material. Our siblings are important to us emotionally and psychologically. We are bound to them on some level throughout our lives; thus, they will appear in our dreams in many different forms. We learn important lessons about ourselves through our brothers and sisters. They are a reflection on us, and we can not escape their presence and their love, hate, or any other emotion. If you have many unresolved issues with your siblings, it is likely that they will frequently appear in your dreams. *See also:* People

Skeleton

You can't get around the fact that bones are symbols of death. If you are dreaming about a skeleton, it does not necessarily mean that you are dreaming about physical death. This is a good dream because it is telling you that you may need to begin "filling up" with feelings, adventures, work, or general enthusiasm for life. It may be that your style of living and relating to people has been "bare to the bone" and your soul can't take it any more! So, lighten up psychologically; eat the fruits of life and fatten up!

Smell

At times you may experience the sense of smell in your dreams. The smell could be environmental. If there is a strong smell in your sleeping environment, you may perceive it and incorporate it into your dream. Otherwise, the smell in your dreams is triggered by a memory. You may be associating your dream experience with a pleasant or unpleasant order. For example, if you are dreaming about your mother, you may smell the aroma of a food she once cooked. The smell may trigger emotions and reflect the general quality of the experience in your dream.

Smoking

It is very common for ex-smokers to dream about smoking. This type of a dream could be called wish-fulfillment or a compensatory dream. The smoker misses smoking. He cannot smoke during the day, and therefore he smokes in his dreams. If you are dreaming about being surrounded by other people's smoke, you may be experiencing some confusion and anxiety in daily life or in regard to a particular situation. Smoke or smoking usually depletes people of energy and hampers one's ability to think clearly and act directly with the issues at hand. *See also:* Cigarettes

Smothering/Strangling/Choking

Dreaming that you are having difficulty breathing and are in danger of dying as a result may carry important messages for the dreamer. This type of a dream experience is usually very frightening, and at times people are awakened from their dream due to the fear. This dream may have several different explanations and the catalysts may be forces from either within the individual's emotional and psychological makeup or circumstances on the outside of the individual. The suffocation is either due to internal forces or an external situation. The dreamer may experience great difficulties when it comes to free self-expression. They may have difficulties in expressing their fear, anger, love, or any other powerful emotion and be literally choking on them in their dream. Choking in your dream suggests that you are having problems in communicating your thoughts, needs, and feelings. Additionally, smothering may imply that the dreamer cannot accept certain situations in life and is feeling suffocated by a current problem. Accurate interpretation of this dream requires consideration of all the details in it; think about your daily life and those things that cause you great stress and restrict your freedom. Finally, try to connect your dream with your daily life experiences and unlock the symbolism that the dream holds for you.

Snake

In some cultures, snakes are highly regarded and symbolize the ability to transcend into higher levels of consciousness or into areas of knowledge that exist outside perceived time and space. In the pre-Christian days, snakes were considered symbols of fertility, healing, and nurturing (the healing serpent representing a god). Post Adam and Eve, snakes are often considered symbols of temptation and evil, anger, and envy. Snakes emerging out of the ground may represent your unconscious or repressed materials coming to your conscious mind. Freud thought that the snake was a phallic symbol. It is amazing how many people have snake dreams! Most snake dreams seem to be disturbing and they leave the dreamer feeling anxious and afraid. There are no simple interpretations to the snake dreams. Each dreamer must consider his own situation and all of the details of the dream. Sometimes snakes may be phallic symbols, and other times they represent negativity in our lives that hampers our progress and constantly threatens us. In the long run the snake may be a positive symbol; it may represent difficulties that lead us to the center of personality and result in feelings of completeness.

Snow

Snow symbolizes chilled and unexpressed emotions or emotions that have been repressed for an extended period of time. The snow in your dream suggests that you or someone else is emotionally cold, unresponsive, and indifferent. Clean, white snow may represent innocence, truth, peace, and relaxation. Virgin snow, as you may see it covering a beautiful landscape, may represent new beginnings or a new way of seeing things, and dirty snow may represent guilt. In literary works such as "Stopping by Woods on a Snowy Evening" and "For Whom the Bell Tolls," snow represents death. *See also:* Ice

Soap

Some dream symbols are more difficult to interpret than others. Using soap in a dream seems to have obvious connotations, a need for cleansing and purification. Consider all of the details of your dream and think about what needs to be cleaned or refreshed. Washing with soap in your dream could refer to the cleaning up of your physical environment, your thoughts and feelings, or the resolution of a particular situation in life.

Spider

Some believe that the spider is symbolic of an unkind and sneaky individual. Are you the spider building a web, or are you being dragged into one? A spider's web may represent entanglement and the general complexities of life. Depending on the details of the dream, it could also symbolize a smothering individual. Ironically, very old dream interpretations say that the spider is an omen of good luck! Alternatively, Carl Jung felt that the spider's web was a symbol of wholeness due to its formation (circular shape), construction, and complexity. As a "mandala," the spider web might hold valuable meaning for the dreamer, and symbolize an integration of the dreamer's personality, leading to greater self-awareness and resulting in feelings of completeness. Therefore, the spider and his web may be considered profound and spiritual dream symbols that call for greater self-understanding and encourage us to derive meaning and satisfaction from the intricate framework and interplay of life.

Sport

Playing sports may represent some aspects of the way that we run our lives, or may refer to internal struggles where one part of the dreamer's psyche or personality is attempting to "win" over another. At times life is like a challenging sport. We compete, try to win, and attempt to develop our abilities so that we will succeed. In the dream, the outcome of the game may say something about how well we are doing. Do we feel competent and successful, are we playing fair, or is the sport more competitive than what we are comfortable with? In order to understand the dream, consider the details and attempt to identify what in daily life creates similar emotions. All sports and games have specific rules and boundaries. Your performance within this framework may represent the struggle against inner conflicts such individual fears and weaknesses, or may be referring to a pragmatic problem or situation at work or in your relationships.

Stairs

When interpreting this dream, try to remember your feelings upon awakening. Going up and down the stairs could mean several different things. It could represent changes in consciousness, movement from one inner plane to another, or a change in understanding. In a more material sense, it could represent a rise or fall in economic or social status and the general efforts that are required to accomplish life's small and large goals. Climbing may represent an achievement of your ambitions and a movement in a positive direction. Descending may symbolize your doubts or a period following hard work and achievement of a significant goal. Generally, dreaming of ascending a stairway connotes movement in a positive direction while descending is indicative of a down period or negative flow of ideas or actions. *See also:* Climbing

Stalking

Many people have unpleasant dreams of being chased and/or stalked. If the dreamer has these issues in her daily life, then the fear experienced during the day may be entering her dream state. However, most people that have a dream about being stalked are not stalked in reality. The dream is symbolic and brings up issues regarding persisting problems or prevailing difficulties. The dream could represent one side of the dreamer's personality attempting to catch up with the other. For example, if the dreamer is doing something hurtful to himself or has a bad habit or addiction, the stalker in the dream may represent that negative part of the dreamer's personality or life. The dream stalker could represent your conscious, a prevailing problem, or a goal that you have been putting off and unable to pursue.

Star

Old dream interpretation books say that seeing stars in your dream means that your wishes are going to be fulfilled. Even from a more pragmatic point of view, stars seem to be positive dream symbols. They could represent insight, luck, fortune, and the mysteries of the universe. Stars represent those wonderful things that we aspire to but have difficulty obtaining. To follow a star is to follow a dream, an insight, or your intuition to a more desirable location or position in life. Thus, stars in your dreams could also symbolize internal or external guidance and truth.

Stealing

People steal for many reasons: if they are poor and feel like they have no other alternative, if they do not want to put the time and the effort into earning what they need (needs could be emotional as well as material), if they have a compulsion to steal. Stealing alludes to moral questions in the dream's psyche. Consider all of the details of your dream and try to understand why the stealing is taking place. Are people taking from you without your permission, or are you trying to reap the benefits of that which you did not earn? The message from the unconscious may be that of self-evaluation, neediness, and morality. The understanding of this dream may bring you closer to understanding your deeper needs which will ultimately lead to greater happiness.

Storm

Everything in our life is a reflection on us and this holds true in our dreams. The storm in your dreams may be a reflection of some difficulty in your life. Consider all of the details and notice if you took shelter from the storm or were you swept away by it. Did the storm pass you by, were you safe, or did you suffer? All of us experience difficulties in life and our dreams make an attempt to bring us into awareness and out of denial. Think about the storms in your life, how you will weather them, and what you can do to make them subside.

Stranger

The interpretation of seeing and interacting with a stranger, or strangers, in your dream depends on the details of your dream and on your personal belief system. Some Eastern cultures believe that the strangers in your dreams are spirits from another dimension. These spirits may be teaching you lessons or giving you specific messages. The more modern approach to interpreting a dream with strangers in it suggests they represent different sides or unfamiliar aspects of our personality. The best way to tell is to "check inside" and simply try to understand the message of this dream. Whether the message is coming from your unconscious or from a different reality might be irrelevant. The lessons gained through a dream are far more important then where they came from. Just remember: The mind that dreamt the dream also knows its source and meaning (and that is YOUR own mind). *See also:* People

Submarine

All vehicles appear to symbolize the way that we maneuver, or get through, a segment of our life's journey. A submarine is a powerful moving machine that travels through deep waters. Deep waters represent our emotions and our unconscious. A submarine could represent the way in which we are navigating through our emotional waters and deal with the materials that are coming up from our unconscious. A submarine can have negative or positive connotations. It could suggest that you are feeling strong and are prepared to aggressively deal with whatever issues and emotional concerns arise in your life. On the other hand, the submarine as a dream symbol could be suggesting that you are overly guarded and defensive and are currently not open to airing personal issues.

Subway

Interpretation of subways is based on your experience with this mode of transportation. If you regularly use the subway, you may need to look at the other parts of the dream more carefully. If the subway is not a regular part of your daily routine but is the primary dream image, then you can consider it to be symbolic of the way that you navigate through your own emotions and hidden parts of self. The subway is under the ground and represents the unconscious parts of self. All of us interact on conscious and unconscious levels. We have intuitive feelings and unspoken understanding that direct our lives as much as the obvious and fully conscious things. Consider the subway ride in your dream and try to understand what it is conveying to you about your more subtle navigation through ongoing life experiences. *See also:* Train

Suicide

At a first glance this dream seems to be all negative. One would think that it connotes self-hatred, deep depression, "giving up," and other such negative thoughts and feelings. At times this may be the interpretation, and if this is so for you, please confide in a friend or a loved one and seek professional help. However, there is a lighter and much more positive interpretation of this dream. It could suggest that the dreamer is making progress and is becoming a more "integrated" person. All of us have many aspects to our personality and our character. Dreaming that you are committing suicide may be symbolic of you "killing" one aspect of yourself. Possibly an aspect of self that is hurtful. For example, if you were a smoker and you stopped smoking in your dream, you may need to "kill" the smoker in yourself; if you see a stranger committing suicide, that may represent another part of you. You may be getting rid of an unnecessary and useless part of yourself, and you may be starting a new and a better way of doing things. If you see someone that you know committing suicide, the dream may be symbolic of your perceptions and concerns about that individual. Either way, the dreamer may be experiencing stress, anxiety, and doubt, so lighten up and try to have more positive thoughts during the day.

Sun

The sun sustains all life on Earth. When you see it in your dreams, it suggests that you are being nurtured and sustained by your environment and your life choices. It could also represent a spiritual force or the light of God. Sunrise may indicate new beginnings and a new wave of energy, while sunsets suggest a period of closure and completion. Sunlight in your dreams is never a negative symbol. Light always symbolizes or indicates consciousness and may connote masculine energy. Its presence, even in the most disturbing dreams, has a reassuring quality. Old dream interpretation books say that sun shining on you is an omen of good fortune and good will.

> *"It is the classical symbol for the unity and*
> *divinity of the self; source of life and the*
> *ultimate wholeness of man*
> —Carl Jung

Swimming

If you are swimming in your dream, you are most likely swimming through the "ocean" of your unconscious and through the "sea" of your emotions. The ease with which you are doing this activity will give you clues as to how well you are navigating through those very complex parts of yourself. Are you out of your depth or winning a race?

Table

A table suggests assimilation, or the "coming together" of varying parts of the dreamer. It could be that you are working on becoming aware of your own multi-dimensional nature and are attempting to become a more harmonious individual. The table usually represents nourishment, friendship, and unity. When interpreting this dream consider the primary function of the table in the dream as well as its shape and those who have gathered around it. Most people can make many associations with this piece of furniture. It could represent emotionally charged events, such as a family dinner, contractual negotiations, or pleasant/unpleasant meetings. The emotional reactions to the situation in this dream will lead you to its interpretation.

Tattoo

Tattoos may represent those things in our lives that seem only "skin deep" but may be interesting and fun. They could represent our thinking, our playful ways, and our seemingly unimportant habits. As time progresses, we may realize that our passing fads have become permanent. Thus, a tattoo may be symbolic of something that we inflict on ourselves, is permanent if not deep, and generally carries with it some negativity.

Teacher

The meaning of this dream depends on your own experiences with teachers or teaching and, of course, the circumstances in your dream. The dream could be addressing your issues with authority and approval. Also, you may have a need for guidance and new learning. *See also:* School

Teeth

Dreaming about teeth is very common in all cultures and age groups. Most dreams about teeth leave people feeling uneasy and anxious. Consider the overall content and context of the dream and note if you are having dental problems before making interpretation. Teeth usually symbolize power and/or control. Animals use their teeth for defense and nourishment and show their teeth when angry. Humans often display similar behaviors. Look and see if you are losing or abusing power and control in any area of your life (especially if you are losing teeth in your dream). Old dream interpretations say that dreaming about teeth is a bad omen that suggests financial difficulties.

Telephone

In our dreams the telephone could be a symbol with which we are expressing a desire to communicate with ourselves and with others. Our unconscious and/or intuition may be trying to give us messages that we have been unwilling to listen to. If you don't want to answer the ring, ask yourself why.

Theater

Theaters may be a metaphor for our physical lives. To paraphrase Shakespeare, life is a stage and we are merely trying to make the best of it. Maybe in your dreams you are acting out some of your personal issues and concerns. Think about the details of your dream and what is going on in the theater. Is it a comedy or a tragedy? Are you having fun, or are you very uncomfortable or bored? All of these will give you clues in regard to the meaning of theater-based dreams.

Tidal Wave

Tidal waves or tsunamis suggest that you may be in a period of emotional upheaval. Anxiety, stress, and unconscious materials may be coming to the surface and affecting your daily moods. Giant tidal waves from your dream may be symbolic of current emotional unhappiness and psychological stress that may be threatening to destroy or uproot you. The outcome of this dream could reveal to you how much strength you have to "ride out" this storm. If you are not consumed, or you survived the tidal waves of your dream, be assured that you will survive the challenges of life and living. *See also:* Waves, Water, Ocean

Tiger

This large and very beautiful cat can symbolize femininity, power, anger, unforgiving vengeance, great force, and cunning. Tigers cannot be ignored, and usually they get exactly what they go after. Consider all of these characteristics and try to see if they apply to your or anyone else's current mood or character. *See also:* Animals and Cats

Tongue

A tongue is used for communicating, nourishing the body, and giving or receiving physical pleasure. After considering the details of your dream, see into what category your dream message may fall. Are you afraid of gossip or a "harsh" tongue, or do you have other concerns in regard to this body part? The extended tongue can be a symbol of mockery, lustfulness, exhaustion, or thirst. Consider your current needs and see if any of them are being addressed in this dream.

Tornado

A tornado is a violent storm in nature, and it may represent violent emotional storms in your dreams. If you have reoccurring tornado dreams, consider the emotional changes in your life and also the amount of anger and rage that you may be currently experiencing. Tornadoes could also represent disruptions and upsets in you immediate environment and specific or current issues that may be overwhelming.

Train

This dream symbol can be very complicated and its meaning is specific to the dreamer (as all dream symbols are). If you normally take the train to work and it is a part of your daily experience, closer attention should be paid to the other details of the dream. Going on a train ride may be symbolic of your life's journey. If you are the engineer, you may be reassuring yourself in the dream state that you are in control of a specific situation or life in general. The train could also be symbolic of your need to move on and to do things in an orderly and sequential manner. Freud said that the train is usually a phallic symbol and that a train going through a tunnel represents intercourse. Freud also said that there are other possibilities to this symbol. For example, if you missed the train in your dream, you may be fearful of missing important opportunities. Jung thought that the train ride represented the way a person moves and behaves just like everyone else and that you the dreamer may be striving for wholeness.

Travel

Many people dream of traveling in planes, cars, trains, or motor bikes. Traveling seems to be one of the most common dream themes. It is representative of our journey through life. These dreams could represent your current movement toward goals or passage through life. Difficult traveling conditions such as a dark road, a bad storm, or an accident in a car or other vehicle may be symbolic of the difficulties that we experience in our daily journey through life. Other times, dreaming about traveling to a fun place and having a great time could be a form of compensation or wish-fulfillment. This type of a dream can be an escape from our daily life and form of transcendence into a beautiful dream world. If you are constantly having dreams about traveling, take a closer look at the current situations in your life. Are things going well, or are they more difficult than you would like them to be? Are your dreams a form of escapism and entertainment, or are they reassuring you that life is an adventure and you must keep moving forward? *See also:* Journey, Car, Road, Train, Airplane

Tree

The tree in your dream is you. The health, size, and overall quality of the tree is indicative of how you feel about yourself. This interpretation is to be made only when the tree is the focal point of the dream. Also, consider whether the tree is alive with leaves, flowers, or fruit, or if it's barren. You may see trees in your dream as a part of a landscape or as a secondary symbol. At those times, consider all of the details, as they may have different interpretations than the one just given.

Tunnel

When interpreting this dream, consider all of the details and the quality of your experience. Did you see a light at the end of the tunnel, or were you trapped in a tunnel and unable to determine your location? The tunnel could represent a variety of things. If it was not an unpleasant experience, it may symbolize a transitional period and a passage into new levels of understanding or ways of living. Freud thought that any tunnel-like object represented the vagina. A tunnel in a dream may also be a symbol representing the archetype of the feminine.

Turtle

These animals hold interesting symbolism. Most people loved turtles in childhood and some do in adulthood. The ideas that they convey are those of steadfastness and caution. They move and change very slowly, and in your dream about them, you may be expressing some of your reluctance to forge ahead. The turtles have strong protective shells, which may also be symbolic of your defense mechanisms or the real life protection with which you have surrounded yourself.

Twins

If your dream entails giving birth to twins, or if you are dreaming about baby twins, please see "birth." Twins in astrology represent opposites, and we may use this symbolism to explain our dream. The twins could suggest a duality in thoughts, ideas, feelings, or states of consciousness. The details of the dream will give you a clue to whether or not these varying aspects are in harmony or in conflict with each other. The twins could also represent the balance that is extremely important to our emotional and psychological health. Old dream interpretation books say that dreaming about adult twins foretells of "double trouble followed by double joy."

Umbrella

In dreams, umbrellas usually symbolize the device that the conscious mind uses to protect itself from the unconscious. Umbrellas might symbolize our unwillingness to deal with negative emotions, psychological baggage, or trauma. If the umbrella is opened, you may be protecting yourself from unconscious materials. If the umbrella is closed, then you may be prepared and be willing to deal with the unfamiliar psyche. Old dream interpretations say that the umbrella is the symbol of security. If the umbrella is broken or turned inside out, your ultimate achievement is possible but delayed.

Uniform

Seeing yourself wearing a uniform in a dream suggests that you have identified with a larger group, a movement, or an organization that requires you to conform and carry out its ideology. This may be positive or negative depending on the associations made and the kind of uniform that you are wearing. The issues expressed in this dream might be about self-identity, conformity, or responsibility (duty). The unconscious is pointing to the possibility that your individuality has been covered up and is being unnoticed because you are functioning as a member of a group and not as an individual.

Uranus (Ouranos)

In mythology, Uranus is the sky-god and the personification of heaven. He represents the undifferentiated and limitless potential for growth and is symbolic of evolution. The planet Uranus was discovered in 1781. Astrologically, it represents cosmic power that causes creation, progress, sudden changes, and, at times, upheavals and interference. Seeing the planet Uranus in your dream may represent unexplored possibilities and potential. It may be an unconscious encouragement to create change and to progress. If life appears to be a bit out of control and if many unsettling changes are occurring, Uranus in a dream may be a positive sign from the unconscious. It suggests that turmoil can be used to create new possibilities and that in the end things will be better off then when they began.

Urination

Releasing bodily wastes in a dream suggests a need to release repressed emotions and/or anxiety. At times, urination may have sexual connotations. Many people dream about the need to urinate, which wakes them up, and then they realize that they need to use the bathroom. At times, the dream triggers the physical sensation and other times the physical sensation may become a part of the dream.

Vampire

Vampires, for most people, represent powerful and evil creatures. Dreaming about vampires suggests that the dreamer may be feeling overwhelmed in some areas of his or her life and is struggling with negative thoughts, feelings, and actions. You may be currently concerned about ethical or moral issues and be experiencing anxiety as a result. The vampire represents personal attributes or negative habits that drain energy and resources or cause emotional exhaustion. If you are being attacked by a vampire, you may perceive yourself as a powerless victim. Interpreting this dream's message may help you to identify the source of your negative feelings and helplessness.

Vase

A vase as a dream symbol usually represents something personal that has value and beauty. It is a holding vessel for water and flowers, which are both deep and meaningful dream symbols. If you are dreaming about a broken vase, you need to consider the areas of life that seem to be falling apart and need mending. It may be your love life, family relationships, career, or any other highly valuable area of life. *See also:* Water, Flowers

Vegetables

Dreaming about a large variety of foods seems to be typical. Food represents nourishment and pleasure. Interpreting the symbolism of vegetables in your dream depends on how you feel about them in daily life: whether you like them for their taste and nutritional value, or find them dull and boring. You may be projecting a need to feed your body or soul or reflecting on a dull and not very satisfying part of life. The shape and type of vegetable and the overall content of the dream need be considered when making an interpretation. *See also:* Food

Venus (Aphrodite)

Venus, the planet, may be seen rising in the east along with the sun and is known as the Morning Star. It also sets in the west and is the Evening Star. Due to the way this plant travels across the sky, it is often a symbol of death and rebirth. It is associated with the sun and considered to be the sun's messenger and an intermediary between the sun and mankind (between mortal and the impartial). In Greek mythology, Aphrodite is the goddess of beauty and love. The love that she represents is not of the emotional and fruitful kind, but rather lust, sensual pleasure, and raw animal attraction. Aphrodite was able to stir sexual feelings in both animals and mankind and often represents the perverse side of human sexuality. She is the goddess of the house of prostitution. Aphrodite may represent our basic sexual nature before it is tamed and humanized by emotions and spirit. In order to understand the symbolism of Venus in a dream, some reflection is required. Are you full of lust and/or has your sexuality been ignored? Aphrodite may be stirring your basic sexual nature. If you are feeling drained by life, the planet Venus may be a representation of the ability to regenerate and begin anew. Seeing Venus in a dream may be a reminder that there is an abundance of internal energy and resources accessible to all who tap into it.

Violence
Research shows that most dreams are unpleasant. Violent dreams are relatively common and may be a reflection of the confusion and conflict that the dreamer experiences in daily life. Dreams with violent themes suggest that the dreamer has unconscious negative emotions such as fear, anxiety, and anger. If you are not dealing with these feeling consciously, your dreams are compensating and bringing into awareness the need for honest reflection and emotional balance in daily life.

Volcano
Volcanic eruptions in dreams usually represent our erupting emotions. Feelings that you may be harboring during the day might take the form of a volcanic eruption in a dream state. The unconscious psyche may be releasing positive or negative feelings in the safety of a dream (i.e., strong sexual feelings, passion, anger, rage, and fear). Superstition-based dream interpretations say that pouring lava is a warning about poor health.

Vomit
Vomiting in a dream may represent those things in life that cause you emotional stress, repulse you, and make you ill. This dream suggests that you are rejecting a thought, idea,

feeling, or circumstance, and that fast, almost violent, cleansing is required. Examine your daily reality and try to identify matters that would cause such a strong physical reaction. Superstition-based dream interpretations say that vomiting in a dream symbolizes reversals, so if you are short of money you may have a stroke of good luck and your financial situation may improve!

Walk

Many people see themselves walking along in a dream. It is very important to remember where you were walking to and if the walk was difficult or not. The way we move in dreams, or the means of transportation, may represent how efficiently we maneuver and progress on our own personal life journey. Also, is the means of transportation appropriate for the journey? For example, are you walking to your neighbor's house or across the desert? Jung thought that if in your dream you are walking to no specific destination, it may represent a personal search and a succession of changes that one experiences in life. In order to understand the dream, considers whether you were walking around aimlessly or were swiftly going to a particular destination?

Walls

Walls as dream images are generally considered obstacles and sources of isolation or confinement. Some people are emotionally guarded and feel unable to express themselves freely. If you are such a person, this dream symbol might be pointing to the walls that you have built around yourself. Additionally, if you are experiencing challenges and seemingly impenetrable difficulties in daily life, the wall in your dream may be a reflection of those factors. Consider your current situation and attempt to identify the source of the walls in your dream. Climbing the wall suggests that you are becoming prepared for or are able to overcome difficulties and/or challenges.

War

Dreaming about a war or a battle suggests that the dreamer has internal conflict. One part of personality or psyche may be battling with another for control, and the dream reflects this internal war. Another reason for dreaming about war is that you may be faced with a situation that requires you to be aggressive or assertive and to come to terms with opposition. War veterans and others who have experienced war first hand may, from time to time, have such dreams based on memory and trauma.

Water

Water is a very common but powerful dream symbol. Its meaning varies with the details and the mood of the dream. Water is a deeply spiritual symbol representing the "water of life" or the "flow of life." Large bodies of water usually represent our unconscious minds and/or soul experiences. Water symbolizes emotions (rough, smooth, clear, murky, etc.). Freud thought that since fluids are involved in sexual activities, at times, water in dreams has sexual connotations. *See also:* Ocean, Rain, River

Waterfall

Water generally represents the unconscious and the emotions. A waterfall is a positive dream symbol that suggests a cleansing of negative emotions or psychological issues. Just a simple visualization or a daydream of standing in a waterfall makes a person feel energized and refreshed. If the

waterfall in your dream is overwhelming or too powerful
for you to enjoy, it may represent emotional energy and unconscious drives that are very difficult to effectively cope
with on the conscious level. *See also:* Water

Waves

The waves in dreams may represent emotional fluctuations.
If you are currently experiencing a period of tranquility and
peace, you may be dreaming about calm waters and gentle
ocean waves. This dream suggests that you may be gathering
energy and recharging emotionally. However, more commonly people dream of violent and dangerous tidal waves.
Tidal waves or tsunamis suggest a period of emotional upheaval. Anxiety, stress, and unconscious materials may be
coming to the surface and affecting your daily moods. Giant
tidal waves may symbolize current emotional unhappiness
and psychological stress, which are threatening to destroy
you. The outcome of this dream may reveal how much
strength you have to "ride out" personal storms. For example, surviving the tidal wave suggests that you have enough
strength to overcome challenges and drowning that you
may be "in it over your head" and should seek assistance.

Wedding

Dreaming about getting married or being in a wedding is
relatively common. If your biological time clock is ticking
away and you are anxious to get married, this dream may be
a form of wish-fulfillment. However, a wedding or a marriage in a dream is a profound and very personal symbol. It
usually represents the harmonious integration of the
dreamer's personality or psyche (i.e., the coming together

of masculine, feminine, shadow, anima, physical, spiritual, unconscious, and/or conscious components). The marriage in your dream may represent the union of the different sides of your own character. This is a positive dream symbol because it suggests a degree of self-awareness and integration. Many people dream about weddings during times of stress and difficulty. Based on superstition, some cultures believe that dreaming of a wedding is a negative omen that generally represents a period of grief and possibly death.

Weeds

Weeds as dream symbols represent neglect. They suggest that the dreamer has not been regularly tending his physical or psychological environment. Weeds are indicative of negativity as well as growth of useless and harmful elements in the dreamer's life. Just as we need to weed out the garden to have healthy plants, we need to weed out the negativity in our minds and lives to grow fully. Weeding in dreams suggests a releasing of stifling and useless thoughts and actions, which frees the mind and improves relationships.

Werewolf

A werewolf is a creature that does not exist in the physical world. He is symbolic of a man who turns into a monster, a normal person who transforms into a bloodthirsty animal. The werewolf may represent something in your life or in your own personality. When interpreting this dream, consider internal and external factors that generally seem normal but have a tendency to transform into undesirable, hurtful, or dangerous concerns in your life.

Whales

For most people, dreaming about whales is a pleasant experience. These huge water-dwelling mammals may be symbolic of the connection that exists between the unconscious and conscious mind. They may represent the dreamer's level of awareness, perceptiveness, and intuition. Some think that they represent our emotional power or are messengers from the spiritual realms. For example, if the ocean waters were turbulent, and the whale in your dream was unpredictable or on the attack, consider the emotional environment in your every day life. Under such unpleasant dream circumstances, these large animals may represent overwhelming emotional or psychological issue and problem. *See also:* Dolphin

Wheat

Wheat is a primordial basic food. The nature of wheat is such that it has been given symbolic meaning in mythology and religion. It is considered the fruit of the Earth, a gift of life and the gift of the gods. It is associated with purity, covenant, and blessing. It may also be considered the basic food of immortality. In Greek mythology, a single grain of wheat was displayed at the wedding of Zeus and Demeter. Demeter was a great mother, a fertility goddess, and was responsible for the seasons. A grain of wheat was symbolic of the cycle of the seasons and the cycle of life. When planted, one grain of wheat produces many on an ear of wheat. As a dream symbol, it may be pointing to your inner "food," or the abundance that the unconscious holds. It may also represent the "plenty" that surrounds you in your daily life. Wheat may symbolize abundance and its ability to continuously regenerate itself. This dream may be a reminder from the unconscious, which tells us that abundance and prosperity is in our nature, as is rebirth of thepsychological, emotional, and spiritual type.

Wind

The wind in your dream could be symbolic of your own spirit or the life force. The wind may represent changes in your life; the greater the force of the wind, the grater the change. A very gusty wind could represent stress and turmoil but also the energy that you need or have to make changes. The sound of the wind and the movement of objects around you are probably what alert you to the wind in the dream, rather than a sensation of wind on your skin (most people don't have tactile experiences in their dreams). The sound of the wind is considered by some to be special because it is a sound of nature and has spiritual significance.

Window

A window is a rich dream symbol. Its accurate interpretation can lead to awareness and a better understanding of a personal outlook on life. If you are looking through the window, pay close attention to what you are looking at. Is it a beautiful landscape or a scene dealing with an experience or a situation from your past? Looking through a window and seeing a beautiful landscape may represent your desire for greater satisfaction and more peace in your life. If you are seeing something familiar, you may be able to perceive the situation in a new way and gain some insight. Some say that a window may represent a time frame. A closed window suggests and inability to effectively communicate and an opened widow may represent desire for new adventure in life. Windows in our houses allow us to see the world on the outside, and the windows in our dreams may encourage us to better see the world within ourselves, as well as the world outside.

Wings

In the United States (and maybe all around the world), there is a renewed interest in angels. People are thinking about them and surrounding themselves with images of them. Angels seem to have gained respect and appreciation, and their wings are their most famous and valuable characteristic. Wings are associated with flying, which in turn is associated with freedom and the heavenly domain. Dreaming about wings suggests that you may have a desire to be "angelic," have a need for angelic protection, or want to transcend current difficulties and problems. Consider the mood of your dream and what type of wings you were seeing. If they were animal wings, look up birds. Superstition-based dream interpretation books say that if you hear a gentle flopping of wings you will hear good news. However, loud and powerful flapping of wings is said to be a warning against illegal or immoral activities, specifically those in which money is involved. *See also:* Flying

Witch

The witch in your dream could represent evil and ugliness or something more desirable such as enchantment. The word witch is usually used to describe a mean and heartless person, and in your dream you may be making associations in regard to yourself or someone else who fits that description. A witch could also represent power, magic, and goodness. "White magic" is as popular and culturally significant as darker witchcraft. However, whether good or evil, the witch always tries to defy natural law and use a shortcut to accomplish a task. Ask yourself questions about the general message in the dream; is it about revealing negative characteristics or about solving your problems and getting what you want out of life by using shortcuts? The most positive connotation of this dream could be that it encourages you to solve difficulties by using creativity and intuition and brings you closer to finding powerful and magical parts of yourself.

Wolves

Wolves may have positive or negative meaning and may represent good or evil in dreams. They could represent hostility, aggression, sneakiness, and ferocious appetites. In some cultures, wolves represent feminine energies and in others masculine. In the Native American culture and tradition, the wolf is a symbol of a mysterious and wonderful teacher. Wolves are considered to be powerful guides who offer wisdom and enlightenment. When interpreting your dream consider your feelings in it and your mood upon awakening. If you were mesmerized and not afraid, then give your dream positive meaning and accept its message.

Woman

Women generally represent intuition, creativity, nurturing, and love. At times they can also represent the negative attributes which are given to women and include physical and emotional weakness, gossip, martyrdom, passivity, moodiness, temptation, and guilt. The content of the dream is to be considered, as well as the emotional tone. If the dream is sexual in nature, look up sex. If the woman in your dream was a stranger and you are a man, she could be symbolic of your feminine side or your attitude about women. If you are a woman, this stranger may be symbolic of different parts of your character or personality. Carl Jung believed that the unknown woman in a man's dream is the anima. It is the "personification of the animated psychic atmosphere; the autonomous activity of the unconscious." Thus, when you meet an unknown woman in your dreams, pay close attention to what she is saying and doing. It is Carl Jung who suggested that women in dreams represent our collective unconscious and men collective consciousness. Thus, the woman is that force or current inside of you that nudges you on and inspires you. It is your intuition and the knowledge that in not necessarily attached to words. Men, on the other hand, represent the active part that uses the information received to create the physical reality of our lives. When the two are working together well we have balance and experience awareness that leads to peace and productivity. *See also:* People, Old Woman, Mother

Woods/Forest

They may represent your unconscious or your "mental space." If you are lost in the woods, it may be a reflection of feelings of confusion and a lack of clear direction. *See also:* Tree, Jungle

Worms

What thoughts come to mind when someone is called a worm? When we are dreaming about these animals, we may be reflecting on the more negative aspects of our own or someone else's personality. Worms are usually associated with weakness and sneakiness. They are blind and generally feed on decaying matter. To associate these characteristics with any individuals, including yourself, indicates that you are seeing a very negative side of them and have a generally low opinion of them (or yourself). If you are dreaming about earthworms, the connotation is more positive because they make contributions to the general health of our environment. Old superstition-based dream interpretations say that dreaming about worms is a warning about poor health.

Writing

Writing is a means of communication. In dreams it may be a symbol of communicating with others, but it mostly represents communication with oneself. If you are writing in a dream or reading someone else's writing, it may be an unconscious effort to become aware of forces or issues in life. Writing is a secondary form of communication. Speaking is more direct and less cumbersome for most. Thus, the written message in your dream may be disguised or may be less genuine than other forms of receiving information from the unconscious. You may be trying to figure something out and this may be the first step in that process.

X-Ray

Dreaming about getting an X-ray or looking at an x-ray may not have anything to do with health matters. This dream suggests that you are ready to look beneath the surface of a current situation or problem. X-rays require focused energy and your dream may be a reflection on the energy that you already possess. This energy will assist you in gaining insight and awareness or help you with problem solving. Old dream interpretation books say that dreaming of X-rays is a dream of the contrary. That is, you will be released from your worries and enjoy good health.

Xylophone

See: Music, Melody/Song

Yard

In daily life, the appearance of a backyard is usually a reflection on the people living in the house. A neat and well groomed yard, with grass and flowers, usually indicates that people living there are conscientious, caring, and have enough energy to maintain their property. The yard in your dream may be a reflection of how well you have been able to maintain your internal and external environment. The backyard points to things that are less obvious and, at times, may be unconscious. It may also represent childhood memories that hold positive and negative emotions and lead to self-awareness. If the yard in your dream is a measuring unit, think about what you are measuring and if any growth has taken place.

Yellow

Depending on the details of the dream, the color yellow could have positive or negative connotations. If the dream has a pleasant or happy mood, the yellow could represent enthusiasm, energy, vigor, and harmony. However, if the dream had an undesirable tone, the yellow could represent fear and the inability to make a decision or take action. *See also:* Colors

Zero

Please refer to the definition of numbers, and remember that zero means none, no balance, and has no positive or negative charge. The zero can also have the same meaning as a circle. The circle symbolizes infinity, completeness, and wholeness, the circle of life and the eternal unknown. You the dreamer may have come to a greater degree of spiritual awareness, and the dream could be spiritual in nature. However, as always, examine all of the details in the dream, as well as its tone and mood, and rule out the possibility of "going in circles" as the primary message in the dream.

Zombie

Dreaming about the living dead may carry a powerful message. If you are "walking around like a zombie," it usually means that you are emotionally disconnected from things going on around you. You may be experiencing unhealthy detachment and be unable to appropriately feel positive or negative emotions. Currently, you may be out of touch and outside of the main flow of life. This dream could positively sever you and help you to become aware of emotional issues and circumstances in daily life that are difficult to face.

Basic Steps in

Dream Interpretation

*A dream is a "spontaneous self-portrayal, in symbolic
form, of the actual situation in the unconscious."*
—Carl Jung, 1916.

1. Write down the entire dream, including all activities,
    colors, people, and setting.

2. Identify your feelings in the dream, from beginning to
    end, and how you felt upon awakening.

3. List symbols that you can look up in the dream dictio-
    nary. The dictionary will give you some ideas, but the
    definitions are very general and may not apply to you
    specifically. It may be very beneficial to look up the
    central symbol of the dream in the encyclopedia or a
    regular dictionary. For example, if dreaming about a
    toad, look it up and find out about its life cycle, color-
    ing, reproductive habits, or mythical symbolism.

4. Do some free association: try to write down any
    thoughts that come to mind in regard to the activi-
    ties, people, the setting, and the emotional content of
    the dream. You can begin by doing free association
    with the symbols that you identified in step 2. Per-
    sonal associations are subjective associations and may

be used to interpret your dreams. At times, objective or impersonal associations, such as a general knowledge about the dream symbol, may be more helpful. Each dream symbol may have multiple meanings and can be applied to many aspects of the dreamer's life.

5. Additional questions that you can ask yourself when interpreting your dreams:

   * Does the dream address any of my larger issues in life?

   * Does the dream point out a specific issue, concern, or situation?

   * Is the dream spiritual in nature?

   * Is the dream mystical or prophetic in any way?

   * What have I learned from this dream; what is its message?

6. Write down what you think your dream means. This may be difficult in the beginning, but with practice you will get better.

7. A single dream may be important and revealing, but it is very pale in comparison to the insight that can be gained by studying our dreams over an extended period of time. Thus, keep an ongoing record of your dreams, read them from time to time, and enjoy the process of self-discovery and the journey into your unconscious!

8. The ultimate goal of studying dreams is to obtain a deeper sense of self. To develop a satisfying sense of who we are and to integrate the various parts of self. To come into awareness in regard to our true nature

and to see with more than our mind's eye. Dreams take us to the deepest levels, the highest levels, the levels beyond our conscious experiences and expectations. Most of your dreams are about you, your characteristics, your needs, your unresolved issues. They are more about you than anything else. Don't ask what the dream is telling you about the future, or about the feelings that others have for you: ask what the dream is telling you about yourself. All dream content goes back to the dreamer with the purpose of balancing the unconscious with the conscious and gaining enlightenment and integration of all parts of the self.

Sample Interpretations of
Actual Dreams

Dream # 1: Blue Cat

ate one afternoon I was standing in the kitchen of my office building and a cat came running in the open back door. The cat was beautiful. It was sleek, short-haired, colored baby blue with a lot of tan mixed in, very unusual. I never saw the cat's eyes. The cat had two tags, one for rabies and the other for identification. The name of the cat was "Sir" something-or-other, some long and impressive name.

I picked it up and yelled for Kristy, my coworker who is a big cat lover (she has four or five), but she had already left for the day. The rest of the dream centered on trying to contact the owners because this was obviously a purebred and expensive cat. I couldn't quite read the phone number on the ID tag. The cat kept squirming its head away. A couple of times it jumped out of my arms. I was afraid it would run away, but I was always able to take just a couple steps and retrieve the cat. Then the cat would nuzzle me and cuddle, as if it felt comfortable and safe with me. It was a very sweet cat. Its fur was very soft to touch.

I decided to take the cat home with me until I got in touch with the owners. Where I lived was a city and house unknown to me in real life. I have two small dogs in real life, and they were barricaded in another room of the house, but they got out and I was afraid they would chase and scare the cat. However, they were only curious and sniffed the cat and then jumped up on the couch and just sat there like statues, one on each end. The cat would alternately cuddle and then jump down. Not because it didn't like me, I sensed; it just wanted to explore.

I was still very concerned with getting in touch with the owners, but I was having a good deal of trouble getting the phone number right. On the ID tag, the numbers were all jumbled together and I either couldn't copy them down accurately or couldn't dial them correctly on the phone. All of a sudden on the table there was a document about the cat, and on the bottom was the phone number highlighted in orange. But I couldn't quite read the numbers through the orange. I was very frustrated. Suddenly my friend Rob (we have dated as friends for several months) was there and he became quite exasperated with me. I handed him the phone and said, "Here, *you* do it if you think you can do better." He dialed the number and handed me back the phone. The line was ringing when I woke up.

When I woke up I was mad that I didn't get to find out if the owners were going to answer the phone!

Simple Interpretation

Animals in dreams represent our intuitive and emotional selves. In the dream, the cat was beautiful and sweet. You could not locate its owners. It could be because you are the owner of that "cat." The cat is symbolic of a part of your inner self. The characteristics that cats represent can be understood by thinking about their "essence" or the associations that we make when we think about cats. Cats are territorial animals. They are guardians of their space. They are also aloof, and a part of them can never be domesticated. Culturally, in the United States, there is a sexual connotation with regard to cats.

Thus, in your dream you found that special part of yourself—the sexy, soft, and curious you (the cat within). But, you insisted on giving it back to a very elusive and inaccessible person. In your dream, the unconscious locates and hands to you all the positive characteristics that are represented by the dream cat. Those characteristics may be inaccessible to you consciously or in daily life. Also, the last part of the dream is interesting. The color orange is generally associated with the reproductive system and therefore sexuality. The phone number of the cat's owner was highlighted in orange, but only your boyfriend could read it. Maybe you have come to the point in this relationship (or in your own psyche) where you want to and need to be sexy and curious, just like the blue cat.

* * * * *

Dream # 2: Robbery

I have had this dream about 3 or 4 times a year for the past five years. I own an apartment or a house and do not live in it. It is fully furnished with all of my valuables. When I visit this house or apartment it has just been robbed of all of my belongings. It has been broken into because I neglected to lock either a door or a window. I know beforehand that I should have taken simple precautions to protect the premises, such as locking the door or window but I always leave them open. After I find I have been robbed, I am outraged and mad at myself for not taking those precautions that I told myself to take. I am so angry that I wake up and can't go back to sleep for at least two to three hours. ANY IDEAS??????

Simple Interpretation

First, it may be helpful to you to note what is going on in your daily life around the time that these dreams occur. The unconscious generally sends up messages repeatedly until we figure out the message of the dream.

The house in a dream is symbolic of you. You are the house and in you are all the valuables that you need.

This dream could be occurring when something negative is going on in your life. That is, for example, when you leave yourself emotionally vulnerable: when you are not on guard and someone in your life takes advantage of you or hurts you. At times, people that are very close to us, for example, our parents, siblings, or mates, sense when we are feeling good and when our defenses are down, and at those times they choose to bring up hurtful issues or "attack" us for what they perceive to be our shortcomings.

Alternatively, the dream may be a form of compensation. You may be having this dream when everything is going really well and you are very successful—in your private life, with money, etc. In order to figure out what this dream means, you first need to notice what is going on in your life at the time that the dream occurs.

* * * * *

Dream # 3: Menstrual Blood

I look down at myself, I am nude and blood is gushing out from my private parts, as if I am menstruating. I can also feel a mild degree of cramping. The location is nondescript because that is all I can see. What little background there is, is white. My thoughts just before I wake up are "Oh, I guess I'm going to die," but it is very matter of fact.

Simple Interpretation

It is not uncommon for women to dream about menstrual blood. Take notice when you are having these dreams and whether they are occurring just before you get your period.

Dreaming about your own blood is usually a good thing. It suggests a cleansing of some type. Women may have a lot of emotional and psychic material attached to the way their bodies function. We have issues of all kinds that include having kids or not having them. At times, being a woman is very painful and not for any other reason other than our very nature (biological and psychological roles).

Even though in the dream you got the message that you were going to die, death in a dream does not necessarily symbolize the death of the body; the death could be referring to a part of self that needs to go. As we move from one phase of our lives to another, we need to allow parts of us to symbolically die, and I don't mean this in a negative way. The less productive, more destructive and unhappy parts of us should die as we get older and acquire understanding and strength. The unconscious message of this dream may be to let things flow—the flow of life—and that is symbolized by blood. However, if you have something in your life that is draining you and taking up all of your energy, it might be a good time to consider your alternatives.

* * * * *

Dream # 4: Ten of Clubs

*T*he dream started with me driving in my car, and I had a deck of regular playing cards with me. The cards were very large in size. I pulled into some type of store, wasn't clear what kind of store (maybe a furniture store?). I went inside holding my cards and the salesman walked beside me as I noticed light blue indoor-outdoor carpet. I dropped one of my cards on the way out "not paying it much attention." I left as if to drive to the next town and pulled into another store. As I got out of the car the salesman I had just left pulled up and handed me the card I dropped at his store. It was very clearly the ten of clubs. As I thanked him, he looked at me as if to say "Did you notice the ten of club?" As I woke up, I was thinking how nice it was for him to drive that far to return the card. It was as if some kind of message was being sent to me but I have no idea what it could be.

Simple Interpretation

Most dreams are meaningful, although it is difficult to figure out their meanings. I am going to make a few suggestions that might help you figure things out. Also, please remember that the unconscious sends up the same message many times and in many dreams. Thus, if you can't figure this one out, there will be other dreams with the same or similar message in it, which you will be able to interpret or see with greater clarity.

The car represents the physical self and the ego, and the car ride represents a portion of your life's journey. In the dream, you had large cards, which may be associated with gambling. In life, even when we are not real gamblers, we gamble with many things. To say that we gamble is simply to say that we take chances because we are uncertain. These chances could be in the area of personal relationships, a career, where we choose to live, or even simple things such as trying a new restaurant (we take a chance and hope that the food will be really good).

All of that aside, the dream may have a different meaning altogether. A club is also a weapon. A weapon is a symbol of power. The number ten is a nice even number that, as with all even numbers, may be considered feminine. So, in your dream you are moving along and stop to shop. Shopping is generally associated with trying to get the things that one needs. As you were going along, you may have dropped your own feminine power and forgotten all about it. In the dream, the unconscious forces inside of you follow you and tell you "Here is what you dropped and forgot—take it, pick up the power (and possibly some luck) that you have forgotten about."

I hope that some of this makes sense to you. Since I don't know you, this dream interpretation is general. I can't make associations between the dream and your life, but you can. Ask yourself if you have forgotten some of your own inner powers and if you are in need of them currently. The unconscious is attempting to make you more familiar with it and your unconscious psychic energy. This is the primary function of dreams. That is, dreams make it possible for us to become more conscious beings, which in turn will lead to greater self-understanding and more happiness.

* * * * *

Dream # 5: Mysterious Girl

This is how it goes, I am a 26-year-old male and for as long as I can remember, I suppose since I was maybe 4 or 5, I have had a series of dreams. These dreams always take place in different settings, but they always contain the same face. These dreams are so vivid that if I close my eyes for a moment, I can smell the grass, taste the air, and swear, if I didn't know better, that I'm physically there. I have had these dreams all my life and the picture in my mind was of a girl I had never met and didn't know. As the years passed, the dreams became more frequent and more vivid, but the face is always of the same girl, yet it ages as time goes by as well. I didn't know what to think over the years and ended up chalking it up as a fantasy, calling it my dream girl.

Well, one day when I was at work my boss brought in a new employee to be trained and guess what? It was the same girl I had dreamed of since I was 4 or 5. At first, I didn't know what to think, but I was 100 percent sure it was her. One thing led to another, and it turned out that both of us felt that we were destined to be and that fate had brought us together. As time passed, we declared our love and things were going smoothly. The hitch is that right before I met her I had begun a divorce proceeding and was in the mist of all that, which really screwed my head up a bit. I un-intentionally hurt her, not by being unfaithful or anything of that kind, but by being scared and pushing her away.

Then she said she didn't love me and abruptly planned to marry another, saying that we could never be. Thirty days ago she told me she loved me and would marry me, and then that afternoon she told me she didn't love me and now plans to marry another. I am devastated, because to me I have been in love with this woman all my life, I continue to have dreams of her, I see us at different points in life, and I see us old together. I believe this is the woman for me without a shadow of a doubt. Can you offer some advice as to the validity of my dreams? Can you offer some advice, as a woman, to what course I might take?

Simple Interpretation:

Dreams never stop amazing me because of stories such as yours. The first thing that I would question is whether the girl in your dreams is actually the girl that you met at work and fell in love with. Do you continue to dream about her?

If she was indeed the girl that you have been dreaming about, then there are several explanations and none of them can be considered purely scientific. In the dream state we access the unconscious. It is a mysterious place, and we have no direct contact with it. The unconscious realm for some is the place of the soul and the realm that is beyond this physical world and reality. At times, we have unconscious relationships with people. The girl, and now the woman, and you have been having a life long unconscious relationship. Finally, you met up in the physical world and went with it. Because of your circumstances you had ambivalence and did not treat her the way she needed or wanted to be treated. Now she is rushing into a marriage that you feel is not the best thing for her.

At times, the relationships that we have in the unconscious world are just not meant to be in this physical world. You will most likely continue to have a relationship with her in your inner world.

You asked me what I think as a woman. I think that if I really loved someone then I would not marry another, especially if the person that I love is calling me and attempting to make things right. You cannot force yourself on her. All you can do is make your position clear and try to reassure her that you want to build a relationship. If she does not respond to you, then you need to move on. You got involved with her before you were ready. It could be that you also needed time to heal your emotional wounds and resolve issues that led to your divorce.

In the long run, things tend to work out the way that they were meant to be. Thus, the only thing that is important is that we are honest with ourselves and that we are reasonable in our actions.

* * * * *

Sleep and Dreams

$\mathcal{T}$hroughout time every culture has had its own understanding of dreams. The value given to dreams has varied. Some cultures depended on dreams to give them insight and foresight into every aspect of their lives. From the scientific perspective, dreaming and sleeping remained virtually mysterious unil the second half of the twentieth century. Technological developments enabled scientists to study people as they were sleeping. Sleep in general appears to be a problem for many of us. Evidence from large-scale worldwide epidemiological studies have showed that approximately a third of all people in the world suffer, or are prone to suffer, from sleep problems or clinical sleep disorders. As we are giving our dreams serious consideration, we can not ignore their context, which is sleep. Also, as modern people living in the twenty-first century, it is our responsibility to be scientifically informed, and to form our opinions and convictions with awareness. Therefore, this section of the book will provide you with a quick overview of broad scientific facts about sleeping and dreaming.

There is no definitive scientific views or purely empirical understanding of dreams. Dreams are much more difficult to study than sleep is. Many of us throughout the world believe that dreams are valuable and necessary to the understanding of our human nature. To deny a dream is to deny a part of ourselves. Dreams are an instant connection to the unconscious, which is a place of mystery and the unknown, but it can be studied and made personal through dream interpretation. A moderate attempt to interpret our dreams will lead to greater self-understanding and awareness, as well as to moments of enlightenment resulting in greater consciousness.

Consciousness

What is consciousness?

The words conscious, subconscious, and unconscious are very frequently used and most people don't think about their actual meaning. Consciousness is the level of awareness to internal and external conditions, stimuli, and events. There is a continuum of conscious.

Continuum of Consciousness

Continuum of conscious refers to the degree of awareness or the progression from total alertness to total unresponsiveness. The following are short descriptions of different levels of consciousness and the cognitive process associated with it:

Controlled processes

★   At this state we are the most alert and aware. We are in this processing state when we are fully concentrating on a task. For example, when we are learning how to do something new or doing a difficult math problem. All of our attention is dedicated to the task at hand, and we are fully aware of ourselves and our environment. The mind is sharp and it is processing information quickly and efficiently.

Automatic processes

★   The task at hand requires little awareness, and we can do two things at a time. When you are driving a car, singing a song that's on the radio, and chewing gum, you are in an automatic processing stage. You are aware of your environment and of your own activity, but no one thing requires your full attention or concentration.

Day dreaming

★   This is something that we all do and it occurs during automatic processing, when the level of awareness is considered to be low. This is a level of consciousness that can be placed between sleep and full wakefulness. Men and woman engage in equal amounts of fantasizing and the content of their day dreams is similar.

Altered states of consciousness

★   Much research and discussion were dedicated to altered states of awareness. It is a change from normal levels of awareness induced by external or internal factors, such as meditation, drugs, hypnosis, sensory isolation, or sensory deprivation. When in an altered state of consciousness, normal perceptions are not possible.

Sleep and dreams

★   Scientists believe that sleep is controlled by specific areas of the brain, body temperature, neurotransmitters, and chemicals in the blood. Currently there are two leading theories, repair theory and adaptive theory, which have given serious explanations as to why we sleep.

A. Repair theory

★   This is biologically based and states that during the night we replenish and repair those things in our body that we use up during the day.

B. Adaptive theory

★   This theory states that sleep has evolved into an intrinsic part of human behavior. Sleeping enabled early man to conserve his energies and avoid nocturnal predators.

Complete unconsciousness

★   A total lack of awareness that could be due to illness, blunt force trauma to the brain, or any other physical condition. During some stages of sleep, people also appear to be completely unconscious.

$\mathcal{S}$tages of $\mathcal{S}$leep

There are five stages of sleep. A regular night's sleep is usually comprised of 3 to 5 sleep cycles, and most people need an average of 7 hours of sleep per night. Four out of the five stages are without Rapid Eye Movement (REM). During a typical night, as a person goes from cycle to cycle of sleep, REM (stage 5) lasts longer and longer.

Studies with young adults indicated that about 20 percent of sleep is REM, about 60 percent stage 2, 15 percent stages 3 and 4, and about 5 percent stage 1 (Soldatos & Paparrigopoulos, 2005). Following are short descriptions of each stage of sleep:

Stage 1

★ The brain is producing alpha waves as we are transitioning from wakefulness to sleep; this stage takes about 7 minutes.

Stages 2, 3, and 4

★ During these stages you are going into deeper and deeper sleep. Muscle tension, heart rate, respiration, and body temperature gradually decline. During stage 3 and stage 4 the brain is producing delta waves. Stage 4 is the deepest stage of sleep. Sleepwalking and night terror in children occur in stage 4 and neither of these experiences are remembered.

Stage 5, REM sleep

★ It takes anywhere from 30 to 90 minutes to go from stage 2 sleep to REM sleep. The brain produces fast frequency, low amplitude beta waves that are also produced when a person is fully awake. REM sleep is also known as Paradoxical Sleep because the body is in a state of physiological arousal. Heart rate, oxygen consumption, breathing, and eye movement are the same as when awake. The only thing that is lost is muscular tension in the neck and limbs. In sleep studies, 70 to 80 percent of people that were awakened when in REM sleep reported dreams. It is believed that all people dream and that it occurs during REM sleep.

Dreaming

Studying dreams scientifically has been shown to be a very difficult task. Dream studies often include waking people up from REM sleep and asking them questions about the nature and the content of their dreams. The following information has been consistently reported:

1. Most people dream in color.

2. Dreams are visual in nature. Taste, smell, and touch seem to be deactivated.

3. Dreams are more frequently disturbing and unpleasant rather than pleasant.

4. Most common setting for dreams is indoors rather than outdoors.

5. Dreams usually involve motion and action.

6. The length of dreams may vary, but most are as long as daydreams.

7. We dream approximately 3 to 5 times per night during REM sleep.

Dream Theories

In 1977, Alan Hobson and Robert McCarley published research which argued that dreams were random, meaningless activities carried out by the nerve cells in the sleeping brain. They called this theory activation synthesis theory. However, a few years later Alan Hobson changed his mind and reported that it seems that dreams have important personal significance to the dreamer.

Today, some psychologists believe that dreams are an extension of waking life, and that in our dreams we express our emotional concerns and most private thoughts. One clinical sleep disorder is called nightmare disorder. People who have been diagnosed with this disorder report to having repeated disturbing dreams that have a disruptive affect on normal daily functioning. Clinical interviews indicated that the content of their nightmares reflect underlying conflicts, fears, or general personality characteristics. For example, a person with obsessive-compulsive traits may report having nightmares that revolve around not being able to complete a task or accomplish a desired goal. Current psychological literature appears to agree that there is a connection between dream content and the dreamer; that dreams may not be irrelevant and arbitrary.

Dr. Stephen La Berge conducted extensive research on lucid dreaming and wrote popular books on the topic. According to him lucid dreaming occurs only 1 to 2 percent of time during REM sleep. It is the type of dreaming in which an individual is aware that he or she is dreaming. Dr. LaBerge concluded that the purpose of this type of a dream is to make the dreamer aware of something important. With practice we can direct our lucid dreams and improve our ability to navigate through them.

The Two Masters

Sigmund Freud (1900)

Freud theorized that dreams were vital keys to unlocking the mysteries of an individual's personality, motivations, and the overall psyche. To him, discussing and understanding dreams was an important part of the psychoanalytic process. Freud first used the term "interpretation" to refer to the unscrambling of dream content. He believed that all long objects represented the male sex organ and all circular objects or cavities symbolized the female reproductive organs. Some basic components of the Freudian dream theory include the following:

1. Dreams are NOT meaningless or random events.

2. All dreams have causes, which generally come from emotionally charged life events.

3. The themes and issues that are experienced in dreams are so emotionally charged and threatening to the ego that the individual cannot deal with them directly.

4. The dream is a façade which disguises anxiety- or guilt-provoking thoughts and feelings.

5. In order to understand the dream, the individual must attempt to look past the façade and discover the real issue in the dream.

6. Psychoanalytical techniques, including free association, can be used to interpret dreams.

7. The content of dreams is mostly composed of sex, aggression, wish fulfillment, and childhood memories.

8. Dream analysis is difficult because of resistance on the part of the dreamer.

> *"The collective unconscious is common to all; it is the foundation of what the ancients called the "sympathy of all things."*
> —Carl Jung

Carl Jung

Jung lived from 1875 to 1961 and was a Swiss psychiatrist. In the early years, he worked in an asylum and was motivated by a desire to understand the human psyche. Freud and Jung were contemporaries. Jung was fascinated by Freud's ideas about the unconscious and by his theories on dreams. Jung did not agree with Freud on many accounts, and he independently researched and developed an extensive theoretical framework regarding the structure of the human psyche and the nature of dreams. The foundation of analytical psychology is the life's work of Carl Jung. He was a prolific writer and was tenacious in his pursuit of understand the human condition. Jung's work includes conventional and unconventional areas of study such as religion, alchemy, and astrology.

In order to appreciate the theories and thoughts of Jung one should have a general understanding, appreciation, and belief in the existence of the unconscious. It is difficult to explain the unconscious because it is not a concrete object. One cannot hold it, look at it, or examine it directly. It is something like the wind. We can see its affects and can feel it, but we cannot grab it in our hands and examine it. Science cannot study the unconscious directly.

The only proof of its existence can be found in the complex workings of the human mind and spirit.

To give the unconscious validity and power is a leap of faith. I don't mean to suggest that the unconscious is like God. In my understanding, it is not. The unconscious is a very private and individual thing. Our dream material may come from this wonderful place that we have no access to during the day. The unconscious mind may have the power to connect us to other levels, or dimensions, of ourselves and eventually to everyone and everything else, including Divinity. Jung said that the unconscious is not necessarily smarter, but that it holds different information than our conscious mind does. It enables us to see things that are at times difficult to understand and admit. The unconscious experiences that are revealed to us in dreams also allow freedom and mobility that would be impossible to obtain through the conscious mind. In a dream we can fly and there are virtually no limits to the possibilities of our dream experiences!

Anatomy of a Dream

Jung believed that an average dream has a dramatic structure, something like a short story or a play does. The structure of the dream can be broken down into four phases, which can then be used to further analyze and understand a dream.

Phase I

★ At the very beginning of a dream there is a statement of place and the protagonist is identified. Rarely is there a statement of time. This is the phase of exposition where there is an initial scene of action, all of the people involved are present, and the initial situation or problem in the dream is revealed.

Phase II

★ In this part of the dream tension starts to build up. The situation in the dream becomes more complicated. The plot of the dream develops and there is much uncertainty as to the outcome of the situation.

Phase III

★ Often the situation in the dream will suddenly change, or something decisive will happen. This phase of the dream is its culmination or peripeteia.

Phase IV

★ This phase is not always present in dreams. It is the solution to the dream dilemma: the result, or the lysis, of the dream. This final outcome of the dream is a message from the unconscious mind to the conscious. If the dreamer does not get the message, or if the conscious mind does not get involved with the dream content, the unconscious mind will keep sending up the same materials until they are noticed. Dreams are repetitive in their content and message. We are given many opportunities to pay attention and to get involved on the conscious level with the materials coming up from the unconscious.

Spirituality and Dreams

> *"The nature of consciousness is sheer luminosity,*
> *mere experience; it is the primordial knowing faculty,*
> *and therefore it cannot be produced from*
> *matter whose nature is different."*
> —His Holiness the XIV Dalai Lama

It would be impossible to discuss dream interpretation from a spiritual and religious perspective extensively in a short book. It is a topic that deserves its own book. However, it is important to mention that spiritual beliefs and practices, which are often related to culture, frequently influence how people interpret their dreams, and what they think about dreaming in general. Many people are serious about their spiritual lives, and psychology as a science is beginning to discuss the role that spirituality plays in physical and mental health. A famous American psychic, Edgar Cayce was a deeply religious man whose work has influenced generations of people. He contributed to the understanding of dreams from a spiritual perspective. In his writing he said that a typical nightly dream may include one or two of the following functions:

* Dreams give real experiences in the spiritual world.

* Dreams provide a symbolic picture of current conditions in our lives.

* Dreams offer contact with God.

* Dreams instruct us in a lesson.

* Dreams present a solution to a problem.

* Dreams give us a glimpse into the future.

Traditional religions such as Islam, Christianity, Judaism, Hinduism, and Buddhism value dreams in their own unique ways. Many people on this planet belong to one of the five mentioned religions and are probably aware of the value and meaning of dreams from their respective theology. Eckankar is a less known religion with a strong emphasis on dreams. It is a religion of "Light and Sound of God." Eckankar is an ancient wisdom that was reintroduced to the West around 1965 by a man named Paul Twitchell. There are many Eckists throughout the world and they practice their faith quietly but powerfully. They believe in the power of karma and in reincarnation. The leader of Eckankar is called the Mahanta and currently he is Sri Herold Klemp. The Mahanta is the living Eck master, who works with Eckists on the outer and inner planes. He is not worshiped but respected, and his residence, as well as the center for Eckankar, is located in the United States.

Eckankar values dreams as irreplaceable tools for self-discovery. It is believed that by recording and understanding dreams the dreamer gains awareness and increases in consciousness. In the dream state it is possible to work out karma, gain insight into daily problems, see a glimpse of the future, connect to spiritual beings (including deceased loved ones), travel to inner planes such as the astral, causal, mental, and etheric, and to connect to our own souls. Dreams are considered real experiences. Eckists also believe that they are assisted by the Mahanta according to their needs and level of awareness. In the dream state the Mahanta comes to them as the Dream Master and he offers his love and guidance in an important dream experience.

Eckists study dreams throughout their lives, and they do not depend on others to tell them what their dreams mean. It is believed that each dreamer has the responsibility to develop an understanding of his or her own dreams. Eckankar is fascinating and, surprisingly, very practical. It promotes self reliance and philosophically embraces all aspects of human nature and psyche. For more information you can visit their Web site: *www.Eckankar.org*

To conclude the topic of spirituality and dreams, this dreamer believes that at a minimum dreams are tools with which we gain self understanding and have an opportunity to grow spiritually.

Index

Dreamer's Notebook